Mergers
Leadership, Performance and Corporate Health

David Fubini

Colin Price

and

Maurizio Zollo

First published 2007 by
PALGRAVE MACMILLAN
Houndmills, Basingstoke, Hampshire RG21 6XS and
175 Fifth Avenue, New York, N.Y. 10010
Companies and representatives throughout the world

PALGRAVE MACMILLAN is the global academic imprint of the Palgrave
Macmillan division of St. Martin's Press, LLC and of Palgrave Macmillan Ltd.
Macmillan® is a registered trademark in the United States, United Kingdom
and other countries. Palgrave is a registered trademark in the European
Union and other countries.

ISBN-13: 978–0–230–01972–0
ISBN-10: 0–230–01972–2

This book is printed on paper suitable for recycling and made from fully
managed and sustained forest sources.

A catalogue record for this book is available from the British Library.

A catalog record for this book is available from the Library of Congress.

10   9   8   7   6   5   4   3   2   1
16   15   14   13   12   11   10   09   08   07

Printed and bound in Great Britain by
Creative Print & Design (Wales), Ebbw Vale

CONTENTS

A small mountain of books and articles has been published on how to make merger and acquisition (M&A) integration projects succeed. The target audience of almost all of these writings is the integration manager who is facing a daunting project-management challenge. Some are manuals with step-by-step process guidance. Others are structured around a handful of 'tips' or 'secrets' that are supposed to make the difference between success and failure. Practically all these writings assume that many readers are encountering the M&A integration challenge for the first time, and so include extensive coverage of the basics.

With this book, we intend to begin a new stack. Although our topic is indeed M&A integration, we do *not* aim to provide process guidance and our primary audience is *not* the integration manager or others on the integration team. In fact, our target readers are CEOs and other senior managers who are not only veterans of past integrations themselves, but also have available to them highly competent managers to run the integration project. That is the 'you' that is addressed throughout this book.

The management of integration projects has become increasingly sophisticated in recent years. In particular, many companies have become much more disciplined about identifying and capturing synergies, while the financial markets have become savvier about scrutinizing companies' synergy promises. An increasing number of companies announce achievable, well-supported synergy targets and meet those targets reliably.

Yet the managers with the strongest records of synergy capture are also among the most articulate in describing the dangers of focusing narrowly on synergies. They recognize the possibility that an integration that must be accounted a success in terms of synergy targets met or even exceeded might with equal fairness be reckoned a failure from a larger perspective. An apparently successful merger might actually weaken a company in a variety of ways that in the long run – or even in the short run – could outweigh the synergy benefits that have been realized. We call such a merger *unhealthy*.

Of course, the outright disasters that are covered so energetically by the business press are the unhealthiest of all. These catastrophic outcomes contribute greatly to the poor average performance of mergers, and generally fall far short of their synergy targets – if indeed they achieve any synergies at all. However, they are not our concern here. We are rather targeting readers who have the experience and discipline to avoid such calamitous mistakes as wildly overpaying for acquisitions and ignoring the best-practice rules for integrating companies.

When senior managers reflect on a merger after a few years, they do not limit their observations to synergy numbers. They compare the result to the full set of aspirations that led to the deal in the first place, and regularly mention surprises encountered along the way. They talk about the strength of the brand and of customer relationships; the morale and retention rates of managers and employees; the merged company's record in serving customers, introducing new products and services, and meeting quality and cost objectives; the tenor of its relationships with business partners; and the standing of the company with investors and financial analysts. Moreover, they usually comment on such highly subjective factors as the levels of energy and entrepreneurialism that prevail in the merged company.

We have found that asking about a merger's impact on longer-term corporate health rather than more narrowly about its performance in synergy terms can be illuminating. It can trigger a host of retrospective observations about how value was created or destroyed in the integration process. Equally important, the health metaphor implicitly poses a challenge for all of us: Why limit our aspirations to avoiding damage to corporate health? Why not consider the merger as an opportunity to create a merged company that is fundamentally healthier than either of its predecessors – one that will continue to improve its performance long after the project synergies have become a memory? We believe that the higher aspiration of a truly healthy merger is in fact achievable.

This aspiration requires senior managers to shift their attention from their integration managers and teams – who have become so much more effective in recent years – to their own role in their companies' mergers. In general, integration management has improved at a much faster rate than senior merger leadership. To close the gap, senior managers must define for themselves the kind of imaginative and energetic leadership role that is outlined in this book.

The book's theme requires some conceptual elaboration in the early pages, of course, but this is an applied guide to leadership, not an essay on management theory. The bulk of the book therefore concerns specific leadership challenges such as championing external stakeholders and establishing a new performance culture. Leadership is a notoriously bland topic when described in abstract terms. The concrete context for leadership action is everything.

We are assuming that you are now facing a major integration, and must quickly define an effective leadership approach to guide it. We have written a thoroughly grounded book to support you in this. We have conducted what we believe to be the largest in-depth survey of merger performance ever conducted. We have surveyed McKinsey consultants who advised on hundreds of merger integration engagements about the detailed practices and outcomes of each one. In addition, we have brought to bear full familiarity with academic research on mergers.

Most important, we have brought on board almost 30 senior managers with deep integration experience as conversation partners (positions shown below are those held at the time of the interviews for this book):

Argus, Don, Chairman, BHP Billiton Ltd

Benhamou, Eric, Chairman and CEO, 3Com Corporation

Bergqvist, Carl, Executive Vice President, Carlsberg A/S

Boehm, Steve, Head of Wachovia Direct Access and Merger Project Office Co-Head, Wachovia Corporation

Evans, Richard B., Executive Vice President, Alcan, Inc.

Evans, Sir Richard, Chairman, BAE Systems, plc

Harrison, William, Chairman and CEO, JPMorgan Chase & Co.

Hill, Greg, Integration Manager Shell Enterprise Merger, Royal Dutch Shell

Imrie, Alistair, Group HR Director, BAE Systems, plc

Jones, Steve, Managing Director, Suncorp-Metway Ltd

Kaufman, Steve, Chairman, Arrow Electronics, Inc.

Kay, Michael, former President and CEO, Sky Chefs

Krarup, Thorlief, ex Group CEO of Nordea Bank AB

Lafley, A. G., Chairman, President and CEO, The Procter & Gamble Company

Larsen, Lars Vig, Director Corporate Planning and Group Projects, Group 4 Securicor, plc

McGrath, John, former CEO, Diageo, plc

Norby Johansen, Lars, CEO, Group 4 Securicor, plc

Ospel, Marcel, Chairman, UBS AG

Peacock, Lynne, CEO Woolwich, plc and Woolwich Integration Director

Penzel, Dr. Hans-Gert, Company leader of Projects and IT Controlling, Hypovereinsbank AG, HVB Group

Pontal, Jean-François, CEO, Orange SA

Sharer, Kevin, CEO, Amgen, Inc.

Shedlarz, David, EVP and CFO, Pfizer, Inc.

Smith, Mike, Executive Vice President, WellPoint, Inc.

Torvund, Tore, Executive Vice President, Norsk Hydro ASA

Turner, Mike, CEO, BAE Systems, plc

Vasella, Dr. Daniel, Chairman and CEO, Novartis AG

Watson, John, CFO and Chevron merger integration executive, Chevron
   Corporation
Wuffli, Peter, CEO, UBS AG

A book of this kind could not be written without extensive reliance on the
experience and reflections of such merger veterans. They are here not to
provide you with the specific answers you need – much less to offer best
practices for leadership – but rather to suggest the range of possibilities for
action. We believe that you may learn from them as we indeed have done,
but your challenges will never precisely match any of theirs. The leadership
role that you define for yourself can and must be a new creation. Indeed, it
must be re-created by you for each successive major integration.

We have made this book short enough to read on a plane trip – not from
New York to London, but from New York to Dallas or from London to
Milan. To achieve this brevity we have resorted to some necessary short-
hand. When we say 'mergers' we generally mean 'mergers and acquisitions'. (There are indeed important differences not just between the two
broad classes of mergers and of acquisitions, but also between types of
mergers and between types of acquisitions. However, mechanically running
through such distinctions everywhere they apply would result in a long,
almost unreadable text.) By 'CEOs' we usually mean 'CEOs and other senior managers with general responsibility for the success of the integration'.
In general, we have tried to resist the temptation to pad our chapters with
caveats and qualifications that will be obvious to our intended readers. In
particular, we have not attempted to provide guidance for critical legal and
regulatory issues as they apply in various jurisdictions around the world.
(Managers should of course inform themselves fully about these.)

Given the global scale of today's M&A activity, we have tried to ensure
that the ideas presented here are workable just about everywhere. At the
time of writing, there is a spate of global telecoms mergers and of cross-
border banking mergers in Europe. We expect each merger wave in the
future to be more global than the previous one.

A copy of this book – marked up with your reflections on your company's
merger experience and current integration challenges – could form the starting
point for a probing discussion with your colleagues on how to achieve a
healthy merger. Indeed, the ideas that emerge from discussion of your joint
experience may quickly eclipse in direct relevance what we offer in this book.

From our point of view, that is the healthiest conceivable outcome.

Boston   DAVID FUBINI
London   COLIN PRICE
Fontainebleau   MAURIZIO ZOLLO

CHAPTER 1

The Elusive Healthy Merger

Academic researchers and consultants have consistently shown that on average mergers and acquisitions deliver at best mediocre performance outcomes. The typical merger is therefore a bet against the odds.[1]

Readers who have witnessed the deals in their own industries over a period of years are not likely to be surprised by these findings. Informed observers can point to egregious errors that have pulled down the merger performance average. The most important of these is deal terms that have made a merger's economics unachievable from the start. Other common mistakes include poorly-quantified synergies, lack of specific accountability for synergy realization, underresourcing of the integration team, and lack of attention from senior management during the integration.

All of these mistakes reflect insufficient managerial discipline. A disregard for how difficult it is to create value from M&A has always dragged down the averages. There will probably always be companies that grossly overpay and then undermanage the integration of what they have bought.

However, there is now a sizeable group of senior managers who have learned through extensive integration experience that these common mistakes can and must be avoided. Integration experience is much more important for this learning than selection and negotiation practice. Nothing can substitute for the experience of putting two companies together in developing a manager's sense for viable M&A strategies and realistic deal terms. Managers who have been directly involved in past integrations are more wary during negotiations and ask more probing questions about how value will be created.

Some of these managers have compiled remarkably impressive M&A records. They wind up on the positive side of the merger performance curve much more frequently than their peers.

One might expect these managers to be relatively satisfied with their merger performance, but in our experience few are. Deep integration experience actually instills in them a gnawing sense that their mergers are less successful than they might have been. Praise from financial analysts for, say, hitting a synergy target several months ahead of schedule is of course gratifying. Yet post-mortem discussions with colleagues may quickly surface a consensus view that the merging company underwent more strain than necessary during the integration, and that the full potential of the transaction was not realized. 'Overall, that merger was a success – *but…*'

During the integration itself, trouble signs may have been limited to slightly higher customer attrition and the loss of a few more talented managers than expected. Since then other problems may have appeared: The rate of introduction of new products may have slowed down. A quality program may have lost momentum. It may have proven difficult to fill skill gaps in a key capability area. Customers may have come to see the brand as less distinctive. Operating costs may be running higher than planned. Suppliers may have become less forthcoming with sharing cost improvements from new technology. More generally, the combined company's culture may seem to be marked by less accountability, collaboration and hustle.

Even in mergers where there have been few negative effects, valuable opportunities may have been lost. Anticipated revenue gains through cross sales or integration of product lines may be disappointing. The sleepy corporate culture of a large acquirer may not have received a salubrious jolt from the greater entrepreneurialism of its acquisition. Plans to use the shock of the merger event to 'unfreeze' some bad corporate habits may never have got off the ground. Few best practices may have crossed the merger boundary even after the boundary formally disappeared. Hopes that putting two creative management teams together would lead to fresh strategic thinking for the combined company may not have materialized.

In our experience, CEOs and senior executives who are skilled at integration are keenly aware that *synergy targets and a few other publicly announced integration project goals do not give a full picture of the outcome of a merger*. It is straightforward to measure the 'performance' of an integration. Much more elusive is the ability to gauge whether a merger is as *healthy* as it could have been.[2]

A healthy merger makes a major contribution to the corporate health of the surviving company in multiple dimensions such as operating and financial performance, business and technical capabilities, the strength of stakeholder relationships, corporate culture, the pace and focus of learning, and the ability of the company to renew and enhance its strategy. Whereas a merely successful merger looks impressive on the basis of a few early performance measures and milestones, a healthy merger stands up to searching scrutiny by knowledgeable insiders for years afterwards.

Adopting this broader 'performance and health' perspective on mergers requires you to identify the full range of effects that the integration would or could have on your company and to assess how well you are doing against them over time. That of course is a highly subjective exercise. There is, however, no alternative to this perspective if your goal is to maximize the overall positive impact of mergers on your company. Neither the project perspective with its emphasis on milestones and targets nor the financial perspective with its focus on readily quantifiable value-creation is rich enough to support the quest for healthier mergers.

We are not, of course, suggesting that the project and financial perspectives are irrelevant. Far from it. Visible achievement of project goals is essential not just for maintaining the confidence of investors but also for building momentum towards value creation. The importance of value creation requires no comment.

In our experience, however, those senior managers who have been most successful from the project and financial perspectives naturally move on to the performance and health perspective. They aspire to lead mergers that are truly healthy, not merely successful from a project or financial perspective.

> **The best integrators have the keenest desire to go beyond conventional performance and achieve mergers that are truly 'healthy'.**

They recognize that because this is an insiders' perspective it may be difficult to share it with crucial external audiences such as financial analysts. Indeed, many senior managers find it challenging to share this perspective with managers in their own organizations. As we shall see, for example, the impact of cultural change is notoriously subject to contrasting interpretations. Some of the difficult trade-off decisions that you make during an integration may be questioned long afterwards. Even when your colleagues broadly agree with your overall assessment of a merger's health, they may differ starkly on detailed assessments and their weighting.

General managers typically relish such complex judgments, and this is the learning frontier for all the best integrators today. It is one thing for a merger to be publicly praised by financial analysts and business journalists in the crucial months before and after the close. It is quite another thing for members of the top team to conduct a frank exchange about the full effects of the merger after two years have passed and agree it was healthy overall – however much they differ on its detailed effects.

Many CEOs show a keen interest in excelling against this daunting standard. They tell us that surpassing competitors' merger performance and impressing external observers is not enough. They know that they will never achieve a perfectly healthy merger – one without the slightest regrets for lost opportunities or unmanaged risks. They will always leave some money on the table after an integration. Yet they are convinced significantly healthier mergers must be achievable.

But how?

To answer that question, the authors of this book launched what may be the most comprehensive research project of its kind. They brought to this research complementary experience in the field of merger integrations. The two McKinsey authors – David Fubini and Colin Price – have many years of direct experience in counseling senior managers during integrations, and have regular access to colleagues with scores of man-years of additional merger experience. Professor Zollo of INSEAD is a prominent contributor to academic research on mergers and acquisitions and has been training executives on these themes for years.

The initial structuring of the research was based on what we believe to be the largest in-depth survey of merger performance ever completed. We studied 78 per cent of all post-merger management assignments completed by McKinsey across all industries and in all countries between 1996 and 2001. For each merger analysed, consultants completed a questionnaire with more than 400 individual information items covering all aspects of the mergers from strategy formulation through integration. Performance was assessed against multiple objective and subjective criteria.

Building on the results of the survey, we interviewed almost 30 managers who have held either integration manager or steering roles (or both) for major integrations at prominent companies worldwide. Their insights have proven invaluable, and we will quote them heavily in subsequent chapters. They are pioneers in the leadership of healthy mergers, and their reports from the trenches provide the primary support for the book's theme.

Together, the survey results and interviews broadly indicated the theme of this book: *To achieve healthier mergers, senior managers must define for themselves a more imaginative and energetic leadership role to comple-ment the efforts of today's highly capable integration managers and teams.* To put it more starkly, advances in the senior leadership of mergers have fallen far behind advances at the integration team level. It is time to begin closing this gap.

> **The key to healthier mergers is senior corporate leader-ship that matches the excellence achieved by many integration managers and teams.**

To fill such a gap we must ask some hard questions about why it opened up in the first place.

An Underdefined Leadership Role

There are three common reasons why many senior managers fail to define a high-impact leadership role for themselves. First, some believe it is enough for them to protect the company from committing the colossal errors that may lead to merger disasters. Second, the increasing competence of integration managers and teams and the rising sophistication of integration tools and techniques make integrations appear to be a technical challenge that can largely be delegated away. Third, the factors that distinguish a truly healthy merger from one that merely meets near-term synergy targets are so numerous and intangible that it might seem impossible to define clearly what such a role would entail.

Closer examination of each of these reasons is justified for the light it can shed on what ultimately is required to lead a healthy merger.

'Avoiding Merger Disasters is Enough'

There have been so many spectacular and well-publicized M&A flops that even senior managers with *no* merger experience know the types of blunders behind merger disasters. There are big bet deals based on exciting but illusory synergies. Then there are premiums that are so inflated that they are unrecoverable no matter how well the integration is executed. There are also cases where a company failed to prepare adequately for the integration, either due to a lack of integration experience or because it failed to recognize that the experience it did have was not directly relevant for the integration at hand. Finally, there are cases of dangerous arrogance towards one's merger partner (sometimes reciprocated) that inhibits the critical process of thoroughly learning about integration risks and opportunities and engenders destructive friction between the two sides.

These are the big blunders that feature so prominently in books and articles on merger disasters. One could write an entire book filled with big-blunder stories and threaded with the admonition 'Don't let this happen to you.'

Senior managers can take justifiable pride if none of their mergers has ever provided journalists with promising material for a big-blunder story. Yet this is a very limited aspiration, for unhealthy mergers that fall short of disaster status are common. Managing well the risks of significant value destruction is not equivalent to maximizing value creation.

'Integration is a Technical Challenge'

Most senior managers do not settle for avoiding big blunders, and recognize that they must also ensure that the integration meets its formal performance goals – typically embodied in synergy targets – and prevent any major adverse effects such as the defection of major customers or the loss of key talent.

Unfortunately, they often see this as a predominantly technical challenge that can be delegated to their integration managers and teams. This is understandable as the project management tools and techniques become ever more refined and sophisticated. Large-scale merger integrations have indeed taken on the look of complex projects in such technical fields as information technology. Reading some large companies' integration process manuals, for example, is not unlike absorbing the documentation for developing and rolling out new IT infrastructure.

The temptation to delegate the integration challenge away is all the greater if the integration manager and team have substantial practical experience and strong managerial instincts. The reasoning is: 'After all, if they run into some problems they cannot cope with, they will let me know. It is best to let them get on with it, attend the regular steering committee meetings, and keep my door open.'

Consider, however, a merger that has had enough troubling side effects to deny it the status of a healthy merger. Is there really any reason to believe that these could have been avoided through greater technical virtuosity on the part of the integration manager and team? Despite its many technical aspects the integration of two companies is first and foremost a general management challenge. Perhaps no event in a company's history has as many varied and subtle impacts on its corporate health as a major merger.

'No Coherent Leadership Role can be Defined'

In a surprising number of cases, senior managers simply do not know how to add real value. This is so even for many CEOs who have held the integration manager's job themselves in the past and could step into it at a moment's notice. Such CEOs might not be at all clear about what they could do to make a merger healthier. It is indeed a grand paradox that for one of the most taxing of general management challenges – the leadership of a healthy merger – the impressive mountain of integration literature that we have built up over the years has very little to say about what the general managers at the top should be doing.

This book has been written to meet this need. Leaders know that they must do more than prevent big blunders and recognize that an integration is not a delegatable challenge. Yet they may be overwhelmed by the Pandora's box that this opens up for them. A merger can be unhealthy in so many ways! Where does one begin?

The factors that contribute to an unhealthy merger are not narrowly technical, and so do not lend themselves to focused and straightforward management solutions. They tend to be highly intangible, such as deterioration in customer relationships or a loss of focus in a key organizational function such as R&D. Moreover, their emergence is unpredictable, and there are always false alarms. It is therefore tempting to just keep showing up at the steering committee meetings to check for problems that may be spiraling out of the integration team's control.

Admittedly, your role must always include such pulse-taking, because a merger integration is a complex and dynamic process that will throw up surprises for even the most seasoned veteran. However, given the stakes involved in a major merger and the crucial importance of getting a strong start for the integration, it is obvious that a fully defined role that includes anticipation of risks and opportunities is required. Reactive management of variations from plan is hardly enough.

On the other hand, it is not at all evident how you should track the success of your leadership interventions, even if those risks and opportunities are clear from the outset. In the real world of corporate performance, a merger is never an isolated event whose impact can be cleanly separated from the corporate context. A host of external factors affect performance during and after the integration, such as technology developments, moves of competitors and business partners, and fluctuations in customer demand. Within the corporation as well, there will generally be several other initiatives underway, and some earlier ones may be bearing fruit just as the merger takes place. Who is to say, for example, how much of the credit for newly focused business unit leadership goes to the merger experience as opposed to, say, the leadership development program that has been running for the last two years?

Except in clear-cut disaster cases, the impact of a merger on corporate health is always open to interpretation. An extremely healthy merger will lead to a whole raft of positive changes after the integration, but each of them could be explained in multiple ways. You may well have a single aggregate synergy number at hand to simplify the task of keeping score, but if offers a false precision. In fact, as we shall see, leading mergers for corporate health requires a willingness to recognize the value of a whole set of intangible factors – such as the quality of relationships with business partners or the commitment of managers and employees to the new company's direction – that a spreadsheet in the integration team room will never adequately capture. In a field like integration management, where progress towards rigorous quantification has been so impressive, this blurring of the scorekeeping may seem to be a step backward. Yet it is actually a prerequisite for moving forward.

The Leadership of Healthy Mergers

Senior managers create value during integrations by crisply defining and energetically tackling leadership challenges that the integration team is poorly positioned to handle. They continuously ask themselves where the opportunities lie for a step-change in the health of the merger. Then they direct their energies there.

Our research reveals that it is possible to generalize about these challenges. In fact, five leadership challenges came up regularly in our interviews. All five depend upon senior managers' ability to understand the diverse corporate health implications of an integration. In-depth discussion of these challenges forms the body of this book, and in this opening chapter we offer a brief overview of them.

Create the New Company at the Top Before the Close

Successful integrators emphasize the importance of preparing well for the merger close and achieving significant momentum by that date. Many argue that the game may be won or lost in this early period: Recovery from a poor start may be impossible later.

This view is reflected in the currently widespread practice of naming the top team, and sometimes another level or two, as early as the date of announcement of the deal. Yet in many cases this new team then turns to the concrete work of integrating down the line even though its own integration is at best superficial. It is trying to create elsewhere what does not yet exist at the apex – the new company.

As the new top team is the ultimate template for the integration, it must embody every characteristic that is crucial for the success of the merged company. In a deep sense, in fact, it must *become* the new company. The quality of company you create early on at the apex is the best that you are likely to achieve anywhere else later on. Tackling the people issues at the top around appointments, alignment and role clarity will have a multiplier effect across the merging organization and beyond. It sets the pattern for everything that follows. In practice this means that you may need to cope rigorously with these issues at a point when the temptations to put them off or paper them over may be close to overwhelming.

Place the Merger Communications Within the Context of the Corporate story

The importance of communications for merger success has been very well codified. Merging companies often have communications customized for each stakeholder group ready at the announcement. They also have a supporting plan with well-specified communications roles for managers at every level, use of multiple channels, and elaborate feedback and monitoring systems. The 'overcommunicate' theme of the integration literature has been turned into an impressively elaborated communications machine at many companies.

Yet despite all this effort, managers often report that their merger communications are less effective than planned. They often conclude that they simply did not 'overcommunicate' enough, and consequently go on to build a yet more impressive communications machine for the next integration.

We believe that most companies can indeed make progress through upgrading the quality of their communications efforts, but there is often a deeper problem. The 'corporate story' – what the company means for its stakeholders groups, and how they interpret its past and present and anticipate its future – is often neither well-defined nor compelling at the point when the merger is announced. The various audiences of the merger communications cannot place the merger in context if that context is unclear to them. The merger communications thus must bear the double burden of explaining at a high level 'who we are and why we did this merger' as well as at a concrete level 'what will happen and how this merger will affect you'.

The ideal here is to convey the corporate story so well on an ongoing basis – and through actions as much as communications – that the 'who' and 'why' of the merger are evident to all and the merger communications can focus on the 'what' and 'how'. Some companies, particularly those that acquire frequently, have achieved this stage where each merger is 'strategically obvious' (as Peter Wuffli of UBS puts it). If, however, the reach or clarity of your corporate story is limited in a crucial way, then you must put extra effort into communication of it to overcome that limit. If, for example, employees of your merger partner have an ingrained negative view of your corporate story and feel defensive about their own, then you must carefully tailor your communications approach to deal with this problem. The concept of the corporate story can be useful in distinguishing where you have a straightforward communications challenge from where you have a daunting one. It can also help to counteract the deadly routinization of merger communications that bedevils even some sophisticated integrators.

The corporate story, however, is useful in another way besides facilitating communications. The story is also a prism through which value-creation opportunities can be identified throughout the integration. It can play this role because it is in effect a narrative of how the company has created value in the past and will go on doing so in the present and in the future. As such, it is a forcing device for perceiving the merger above the level of

the integration project with its emphasis on the nuts and bolts practicalities
of putting the company together.

Focus Attention on the Performance Culture Needed for the New Company

Cultural integration is the most vexed topic in the field. Here there is practically no consensus around what best practice is. Instead, we find a spectrum of approaches here ranging from an intensive, explicit engagement
with the challenge of merging cultures to a more traditional focus on the
business goals of the integration with limited or no discussion of culture at
all. We have seen approaches at both extremes and at intermediary points
both succeed and fail.

There are two common myths about cultural integration that inhibit clear
thinking about this challenge. One myth holds that the stronger of the two
cultures will naturally emerge from the process in a sort of survival-of-the-
fittest competition, so no explicit management of cultural integration is
required. Unfortunately, under the hothouse conditions of an integration the
less desirable of the two cultures may in fact prevail. Moreover, in most
cases the optimal outcome is more complex than the victory of one culture
over the other. Often both sides have important cultural traits that are worth
retaining in the merged company. In some cases, in fact, the best course for
the merging company is to maintain the cultural contrast for the future.
Many large acquirers, in particular, are rightly concerned about preserving
the culture of their acquisitions.

The second, starkly contrasting myth is that the new top team can readily
implement whatever cultural change it desires across two merging companies, each of which may have tens of thousands of employees in scores of
countries and a dozen or more distinct professional subcultures. This is
hubris of the first order. Corporate culture emerges over time from the full
set of actors in a company. It cannot simply be programmed by the corporate center. Moreover, there is always much more cultural differentiation
within a company than a blithe summary of its culture would suggest, and a
high level of differentiation can be very healthy. Who would want their mar-
keters and their engineers to think and act in precisely the same ways?

We believe the most promising approach is to intervene actively to shape
the cultural outcome but to focus these efforts on what we call the 'performance culture', that is, the crucial set of attitudes and behaviors that are
required to create value in the merged company. The key here is not to dwell
extensively on the numerous cultural contrasts between the two companies.
Doing so could make the merger unhealthy by actually reinforcing the

pre-merger corporate identities. Indeed it might even lead to a debilitating negotiation over cultural traits that has nothing to do with how you plan to create value in the future. As former Sky Chefs CEO Michael Kay told us, you should focus on the cultural foundations for success in the future, and the description should be as concrete, externally-oriented and business-like as possible.

All companies continue to evolve after a merger, and those that achieve significant marketplace success naturally tend to evolve in a way that reinforces that success. During the integration you should therefore focus on creating the cultural conditions for such success. How positively a company evolves after the integration is a strong indicator of the merger's health.

Become an Active Champion for Crucial External Stakeholders

Most integrators in effect divide stakeholders into two groups. There is one set – generally employees, investors and analysts – with whom managers engage energetically in order to secure their support for the merger. There is then a second set – often customers, business partners, and communities – that managers try to shelter from the merger's effects as much as possible. They may need reassurance on some key points, but the general message is that they should relax because the merger will not affect them much in the short run and in the long run might even leave them better off. So the most talented employees get a bear hug, while the best customers get a form letter.

The determination not to burden customers and other stakeholders with integration mechanics represents a real advance, and we applaud it. We agree that they should not be impressed as laborers in the integration project. Yet the two merging companies do interact routinely with these stakeholders, and the inevitable turmoil of the integration process will affect that interaction despite your best efforts to isolate the integration from the normal business of the company. More subtly, as 3Com's Eric Benhamou emphasized, your knowledge of the new set of stakeholders that the merger brings with it is extremely limited. For example, you may have integrated a dozen sales forces in the past, yet you still may be unable to identify immediately the pivotal, tacit features of the customer relationships of a new merger partner's sales force. You never know exactly what you have just bought – at least not like you know your own company – and must undertake the integration without such exact knowledge.

In fact, to achieve a healthy merger it is best to begin with deep humility about what you know in a number of areas. Where your competitors might strike during the integration, which customer relationships are vulnerable, what features of your company's and your partner's brands require the most diligent protection, in what ways your business partners are recalculating their options, what the reaction to the merger will be among relevant governmental authorities and communities – these and a host of other questions cannot be immediately answered with any confidence.

Every integration begins with dangerous knowledge gaps about the world beyond the borders of the merging company. Even where both management teams have profound knowledge of their external stakeholders it will take time before these two pools of knowledge can be combined to form a deeply-shared understanding. This is a major vulnerability, yet many integration plans pay scant heed to the urgent need to overcome it.

What this means in practice varies dramatically from one integration to the next depending on how the merger may affect each group of external stakeholders. In general terms, however, your challenge as a senior manager is to identify those stakeholder groups where the value at stake is significant and to become their active champion. Leadership here requires genuine insight into the issues that may arise beyond the corporate boundary, that is, the ability to analyse corporate health in very broad terms. It also requires real tenacity, because merging companies have a strong tendency to turn inward and make critical integration decisions without robust analysis of the consequences for key external stakeholders.

Identify the Need For and Undertake Integration-Critical Learning in Real Time

Learning is often seen as a valuable objective in integrations that routinely loses out to the even more valuable objective of sustaining momentum. It is so difficult to learn under the stressful conditions of an integration that the standard approach is to minimize the aspirations for learning until after the integration is over. This is intended to ensure that learning efforts do not rob the integration of its momentum.

On the other hand, there have been significant advances in the creativity and rigor with which sophisticated integrators compile lessons learned after the merger is over and apply them to the next merger. The conventional approach is therefore:

Just get it done. Hold off on learning until later. Then make sure you do it better the next time.

This rigid deferral of learning is based on an oversimplified view of the integration challenge. In reality, integration is a learning-intensive activity where a large number of actors need to change a wide array of behaviors. While much of this integration-critical learning is straightforward, some will always be quite difficult. It is no simple matter, for example, to radically modify an integration routine that has proven to be effective numerous times in the past. Yet Arrow Electronics' Steve Kaufman found this unlearning and relearning to be essential for achieving the value-creation objectives of one of the company's acquisitions. At BAE Systems, urgent learning was required to replace a shortfall in synergies with alternative cost savings. In both these cases, learning was actually a precondition for securing momentum rather than a hindrance to it.

Achievement of a healthy merger may well depend on your ability to recognize where the trade-off between momentum and learning does *not* apply. Almost invariably there will be some difficult learning challenges that you must take up in order to achieve the value creation objectives of the merger. Yet few integration plans include any assessment of what these integration-critical learning challenges are – not to speak of concrete steps for meeting them.

Frequently these challenges are daunting because they require that you develop and apply 'corporate self-knowledge'. Even where the logic of the merger depends upon your learning from your partner, knowledge of yourself may be equally critical. The success of UBS' acquisition of O'Connor & Associates was dependent on the bank's willingness to confront the limitations of its own culture. Such hard-won self-knowledge can dramatically expand the range of value-creation opportunities that you are able to identify. Without it, you are trying to put together two companies of which one is new to you and therefore obviously unknown while the other seems as familiar as your own skin yet may be much less well known than you imagine. The pivotal importance of this self-knowledge is the most striking finding to emerge from our survey.

The ultimate people issue may therefore be a merging company's challenge to learn about itself. And the ultimate hallmark of a healthy merger may be that a *wiser* company emerges from it.

*   *   *

Our research shows that these five challenges provide promising opportunities for leadership. For each of them, crossing the threshold from a merely adequate response to an exceptional one can have a startling effect on the healthiness of a merger.

In our prior experience and in the research for this book, we have encountered many impressive merger leaders. However, as far as we are aware, there are no pentathletes out there that consistently excel against all five of the leadership challenges with each integration. In any case, the senior leadership role must itself be tailored each time, so in terms of merger leadership you really never arrive.

Where any one of these leadership challenges is taken with full seriousness – particularly the first one about creating the new company at the top – a healthy merger becomes less elusive. That is our central claim. A perfectly healthy merger may be as unattainable as perfect human health, but in the integration game shifting the odds in your favor is well worth the effort. Within the covers of this short book you should be able to find several ideas that will help you to do so.

CHAPTER 2

Creating the New Company at the Top

Carlsberg's Paul Bergqvist, reflecting on the 2001 integration between Carlsberg of Denmark and Orkla of Sweden, captured succinctly what creating the new company at the top entails: 'You can always have a lot of get-together dinners, but that's not the point. You have to name the right top team, get it structured correctly, define its new agenda and develop trust between its members so they can work well together.' This is your first and arguably most important leadership challenge – one that is far more difficult than a casual observer might imagine.

In fact, some managers fail catastrophically with this challenge, and in doing so provide some of the most colorful copy for business journalists. A dramatic breakdown in the working relationship between senior managers across the merger boundary is impossible to hide for long. The effects of such a rupture may extend to the complete failure of the merger. Indeed, the emergence of 'ego clashes' and 'politics' during the integration is cited as the root cause for some of the most spectacular merger disasters.

Many of these mergers are doomed from a critical moment during the negotiations when the two sides deferred pivotal decisions on the new company. Whatever language was agreed was ambiguous enough to support radically different interpretations. In such cases the managers may approach the integration with fundamentally incompatible perspectives on the way forward. There may even be a sense of betrayal as each side supposes that its understanding of the merger was agreed up front and later disavowed by the other side. Perhaps nothing can so quickly undermine an integration as the conflict between two sets of managers that are, in effect, working conscientiously to implement very different mergers.

Our concern in this chapter, however, is not with such negotiation failures. The argument that the 'real' negotiations around power and purpose can only come after the deal is closed is sometimes advanced in order to shift the burden for achieving clarity to the integration period. However, this is really just an excuse for negotiators who are more concerned with closing a deal than with securing the future of the merged company.

We are interested here in the many cases where a cohesive and effective top team does not emerge quickly after the deal is announced despite a clear outcome of the negotiations. We hear too often that a merged company's top team did not really function properly until far into the integration process. Indeed, in some cases it did not do so until much later. There are some major corporations whose top teams remain loose partnerships between two subteams representing predecessor companies that formally disappeared years ago. Any delay in the maturation of the top team can have a host of negative effects on the rest of the company as decisions are deferred, bad compromises are implemented, and mixed messages are sent to the rest of the merging company.

This is an area where we believe many otherwise sophisticated integrators can and should move much faster. You should strive to *complete* the integration at the apex of the company *before* the close. This is not a detour from value creation, but rather an essential part of it. To get a truly powerful start, you must ensure that your team fully and immediately leads on the basis of the principles and priorities of the newly merged company.

> **To maximize your effectiveness in integrating down the line after the close, you must actually create the new company at the top before the close.**

We make this recommendation even though we recognize that the dramatic growth in pre-close activity in recent years may make it more difficult to follow.

The Rush to the Close

We have yet to encounter a sophisticated integrator that is completely satisfied with how fast they got out of the blocks on their last integration. With each successive merger they aspire to get more things done – and better – before the close. David Shedlarz of Pfizer, for example, told us that Pfizer entered its merger with Pharmacia in 2003 with a vivid memory of its Warner-Lambert acquisition three years earlier, when there had not been enough pre-close legwork. 'So we did a lot more of it with Pharmacia [in 2003]. We used the time period between contract signing and the close to do a tremendous amount of transition planning and communication. We not only had a Day-1 Plan, but also a Day-100 and a Day-200 Plan, each with great specificity.'

Companies that get better and better at integration move from a great deal of pre-close preparation to even more. Many senior managers block out much of their calendars for the myriad planning activities needed to create the integration team and to prepare it for a fast start at the close. They know that extensive pre-close activity pays for itself many times over, so they roll up their sleeves.

From a historical perspective, this is a dramatic change. 'Cold start integrations' – those where nothing much happens until the kick-off event after the close – were common not that long ago. Today they are almost unknown except among companies with no recent merger experience. Steve Boehm, who co-managed Wachovia's 2004 integration of SouthTrust, expressed the sense of urgency that prevails today among the best integrators: 'If you don't have a clear understanding of who is calling the shots, of roles and responsibilities and of the way that the integration team is going to work together from the very beginning, then your chances of success are minimal.'

The trend towards greater pre-close activity has been bolstered by the emergence of innovative ways to share knowledge during this period within legally permissible bounds. There are indeed some legal restrictions (which vary by jurisdiction), but many merging companies have found that by carefully heeding legal counsel a great deal of planning can be done within the law.

John McGrath was the CEO of Grand Metropolitan during its 1997 combination with Guinness to form Diageo, and afterwards the CEO of the combined company for three years. He described to us how much work a 'clean team'[1] could get done in assembling information before the close: 'We lived under an extraordinary regime of lawyers, but we found we could get a third party to collect all the data that we needed: Pricing, every major customer, every country, vast amounts of product data. On the day of completion they dumped the truckload on us and that saved us five months. It was just wonderful.'

Under the competition laws, strictly speaking only integration *planning* can take place before the close. Moreover, these laws restrict the exchange or discussion of some information during this period. However, dealing with this material when it is legal to do so will go much more smoothly if planning has been rigorous and all legally permissible areas visited. We held a pre-close interview with Mike Smith, the then CFO of health insurer Anthem Incorporated who led its integration activities with merger-partner Wellpoint in 2004. Of the 27 subteams that he oversaw, 22 were already able to make the key planning decisions that would guide the complex

integration of the two huge insurers. He ticked off some of the areas of free-
dom that he enjoyed:

> We know what our investor relations strategy will be and who will lead
> it. We know what our tax department will look like, and what our tax
> reporting and tax strategies will be. We know what our treasury and
> investment shop will look like, where it will reside, who will be in
> charge, whether it will follow an in-house or outsourced strategy – and
> we're ready to implement that. We know which underwriting and actuarial
> process will be the new corporate standard. We know which IT shop will
> survive, how we will create the new technology architecture, and how we
> will get there. And the list goes on.

Therefore the notion that little detailed planning activity can take place before
the close is now widely recognized as obsolete. With it goes the pleasant
illusion that the period between the announcement and the close provides a
respite from the demands of merger leadership.

However, as with so many advances in merger leadership, the dramatic
growth in pre-close activity holds the danger of diverting attention from a
critical prerequisite for a healthy merger – the need to integrate the top
team.

Integrating at the Apex

The urgent challenge of integrating two large companies *down the line* all too
often leads to shortcuts in integrating *at the apex*. Even where the top team's
members are selected long before the close, little effort may be made to turn
them into a cohesive, focused team that embodies the company's future. They
are too preoccupied with urgent demands from the business and the integration to give this much attention.

> **There is a danger that integration down the line will crowd
> out integration at the apex.**

The rationale for this is superficially appealing: The top team is generally a
minute part of the merged headquarters organization and therefore accounts
for only a very small percentage of total costs. Moreover, all the revenue is
generated down the line. A top team that uses up its precious pre-close time

on its internal concerns is poorly positioned to move quickly to capture synergies and to protect against such value-destroying shocks as the loss of talent and of customers. Therefore, the reasoning goes, the top team should address its internal issues in a rough and ready way so that it can focus as quickly as possible on value creation and protection elsewhere. After all, what could be more harmful than a top team that is fixated on itself rather than on the creation of value in the new company?

There are so many urgent, concrete tasks to be accomplished in integrating down the line that focusing effort on integrating the top team may seem by comparison to be an eminently deferrable team-building exercise. It seems 'undisciplined' for the top team to spend hours debating its processes and accountabilities when it has a new company to integrate and run.

Many companies therefore settle for a superficial integration of the top team, thus allowing problematic characteristics of the two sides to linger and hamper the movement to the desired norms of the new company. Lack of integration on the top team will be evident to all its members, even if none of them speak openly of it. Indeed, surprisingly often no one will bring it up. As one manager recounted, 'For months we were really two teams, and we all knew it. But we just didn't want to deal with it, so no one raised the issue.'

In the case of an acquisition, the target may be denied representation at the most senior levels of management – even where the acquisition is a sizeable one and was undertaken expressly to add major new capabilities to the company. This, too, represents a failed integration of the top team, even though the effects are less obvious when only one side is represented in the meeting room.[2]

The paradox here is profound: At a time when a successful step change to a new company is the order of the day, the top team may turn out to be a conservative if not obstructive force that fails to set an effective pattern for the new company and sends the wrong signals to employees and other stakeholders. The team that needs to act as the champion of change runs the danger of becoming an impediment to it. This fundamentally crippling effect may occur even where progress in launching an integration team suggests that the integration has powerful momentum. Such appearances can be deceiving. Behind the visible discipline of fast-paced, structured activity lies neglect of the top team's responsibility to integrate itself. This neglect will ultimately hamper integration.

Cases where integration down the line is more successful than it is at the apex are rare. Cases where the merged company fails to create the best possible top team because of 'politics' or squeamishness about hard choices are, however, numerous. The degree of integration achieved at the apex has a profound impact on integration down the line. In fact, the game is often won or lost at this early stage.

> **The quality of company you create early on at the apex is the best that you are likely to achieve anywhere else as the integration unfolds.**

This runs somewhat counter to some recent management thinking. When it comes to change management, it is no longer common to stress the pivotal role of the top team. In recent years the consensus view of how to manage change has shifted from a top-down model to a dispersed approach. Too many top-down initiatives that were meant to cascade down the hierarchy have delivered disappointing results. The usual interpretation is that top-down change fails to work because the messages get diluted at each step of the cascade and at each rung feel less compelling and less authentic.

Whatever the truth of this point of view, in a merger it is not possible to initiate change in other parts of the organization as is done with some other change programs. The change required in an integration cannot be driven from an entrepreneurial business unit, an innovative functional unit or the front line. Too much coordinated, programmatic change must be achieved in a short period of time. The spirit of the whole project is determined at the top. That is where the conditions are set, or not adequately set, for the whole integration.[3]

True integration at the apex of the company meets the change challenge because the top team does not just talk about the new company, or adopt its language and trappings, or act according to its norms: *It becomes the new company in the full sense*. As it goes on to integrate down the line, therefore, the top team in effect re-creates itself. It is not just rolling out messages, or processes, or a set of targets – it is rolling out *itself*. Because it already *is* the new company, its messages, processes and targets deeply incorporate the aspirations of the new company and are seen as to do so by managers, employees and even outside observers.

The top team's smallest flaws and imperfections tend to be replicated throughout the merging company. The climate of rawness that a merger creates among managers and employees makes them very sensitive to signals sent by the top team. Slight missteps, imprecise communications, inconsistent messages – all these get ramified and amplified throughout the organization. Any unconscious reticence to embrace the new company fully will also be detected. There is an organizational equivalent of 'body language' that stakeholders respond to and weigh against the formal communications that talk up the merger. Limited aspirations, poor compromises, and lingering divisions on the top team will be sensed and replicated everywhere in the merged company.

Far from being secondary, to a remarkable degree the top team integration provides the template for integration down the line.

The Ultimate Integration Template

Integration processes today are filled with templates – those myriad forms that integration team members and managers must complete to facilitate the transition to the new company. Such templates capture, for example, the specific sources of synergies and the movement of personnel from organizational units of the predecessor companies to their new organizational homes. This structured mountain of documentation is essential for precisely defining the 'from–to' of the integration. As tedious as this paperwork sometimes seems to be, it has actually contributed significantly towards making the integration of huge enterprises possible.

However, the most important template is not captured on paper. The top team that emerges from the pre-close period is the ultimate template for the integration. In the best cases, it clearly 'documents' the kind of company that is being created and signals senior managers' commitment to it. The result is a cascading series of decisions and actions throughout the company that echo the decisions and actions of the top team, and thus make a healthy merger possible.

In other cases, the template lacks the requisite quality. Weaknesses in the top team are inevitably cascaded throughout the merging company, no matter how diligent the integration team is in pushing for a better integration outcome.

> **For the top team of a merging company, who you are is what you get.**

Put differently, managers and employees must be able to see the future of the company enacted in the behaviors of the top team's members. Yet this is not just about signaling – as important as that is. It is also about the leaders making tough, practical decisions and taking value-creating actions that build the new company. The power of these signals is due to the fact that they are not just signals: They create concrete realities.

The most important of these reality-creating signals fall into three categories: Appointments, alignment, and role clarity.

Senior Appointments

The degree to which managers, employees and even other stakeholders closely watch to see who ends up on the top team is one of the most memorable phenomena of one's first integration experience. This attentiveness represents much more than a voyeuristic interest in the human drama involved. The appointments provide strong clues about the direction of the new company and – more subtly – about the degree of its commitment to its proclaimed course. Managers and employees will of course also interpret them as signals about their own future.[4]

It is important to understand the impact of these signals on each side of the merger boundary. Developing this imaginative empathy is critical, for the signals may depart from expectations in very different ways.

For example, former CEO Michael Kay told us that after Sky Chefs acquired Caterair in 1995 a 'moment of truth' came when the Caterair managers needed to face the reality of the new performance standards. He added, however, that there was a similar moment of truth for Sky Chefs managers because a number of Caterair managers were selected for senior leadership roles. Both of these moments of truth signaled to the merging company's managers and employees a deep commitment to performance. Yet the Caterair managers had a general expectation that standards would be high, and the only question was 'How high?' They were surprised, however, to find that some of their colleagues were senior players in the new organization. The Sky Chefs managers of course knew all about the performance standards. Yet at least some of them apparently nourished the hope that employment on the 'winning' side of the merger boundary would give them an edge in the competition for appointments. It did not.

If you get the appointments right, you may even reach an early tipping point. After that, your chances of achieving a healthy merger soar. Dick Evans of Alcan described to us this catalytic effect:

> Once you get the first couple of layers of the permanent organization named – as long as you do it right – you're already over the toughest part of the integration because you've got leadership people from both companies in key positions, and you already have a new organization. It's amazing how quickly it starts to function as one.

This remark draws on two highly successful integrations: Alcan's acquisitions of Algroup in 2000 and of Pechiney in 2004. Interestingly, these two successful integrations followed an aborted three-way merger of equals among the same three companies. That earlier experience contributed to

Evan's judgment of the top appointments as 'the toughest part of the integration'. It also throws light on how *not* to create the company at the top.

For that first planned merger, the need to achieve balance among the three partners (or at least the appearance of it) drove the decision-making process. For example, each of the three partners was allocated two of the six business groups, irrespective of whether the resulting six appointees were best positioned to carry the new company forward.

Had the deal gone through, Evans believes that the same goal of political balance would have had a host of deleterious effects on decision-making. 'That's probably the way we would have allocated capital and a lot of other things', he told us. Thus poorly handling a standard people issue – the strongly felt need to signal inclusiveness by appointing senior managers in an 'equitable' fashion – could have compromised the merged company's value-creation efforts long after the integration was complete.

In the end, however, it did not come to that. The deal did not go through, or at least not as it was originally structured. The European Union imposed conditions for antitrust approval to which the poorly-integrated top team simply could not cohesively respond:

> It was an ungovernable process with three CEOs, three boards of directors and hidden powers behind the scenes. The simple fact was that we could not agree on what to do. We knew we had to divest one of two operations, but given the dynamics of the group we just could not reach an objective decision on which one. Everybody had skin in the game. There was a lot of jockeying for position in terms of management jobs, board seats – even the name of the company. So at the end of the day it was just undoable.

The inability of a poorly-integrated top team to act effectively may become obvious immediately. For example, when a regulator requires divestiture, sometimes it is obvious which business units need to be divested. At other times, management has some range of choice in meeting the regulator's demands, and the disposals may need to be more fine-grained than business units (for example, at the level of specific assets, business agreements or intellectual property). In such cases, divestiture may be a tough call requiring both complex analysis and difficult judgment. Any top team that has been created through politically 'balanced' appointments is ill-equipped to make a sound decision – not to speak of executing it. In other words, any team whose origins violated the principle of prioritizing value creation is unlikely to create much at any point along the line. Value creation simply is not in its genes.

> **Any top team whose selection does not reflect a central concern with value creation is unlikely to create much value over time – and the whole organization will recognize this.**

Creating the new company at the top is particularly problematic in a merger of equals because managers are sorely tempted to maintain the identities of the predecessor companies. To be sure, the proclaimed strategy usually calls for their full integration. Yet compromises on people issues may fatally obstruct integration and ultimately undermine the merged company's pursuit of value. The resulting mess will often be attributed to 'incompatible cultures' as if the failed integration were the inevitable result of trying to mix oil and water.

Dr. Daniel Vasella, the architect of Novartis, offered a different analogy. He compared Ciba-Geigy and Sandoz, which merged to form Novartis in 1996, to two parents that gave birth to a new company. The point of this homely analogy is a tough-minded one: 'You respect your parents, but you are a different person, not just a replica of them.' Like a new person, a new company must live its own life, not simply re-enact the lives of those that gave it birth. In a host of practical ways, the members of the top team must be able to let go of their attachment to their predecessor companies. Failure to achieve this is a prominent factor in the disappointing results of so many mergers of equals. In effect, the equals never really merge.

Another source of failure to create the new company at the top comes from an unwillingness to face the prospect of job losses among close colleagues who have performed well for years – even though there may be many more job losses among people down the line. In our discussions with John McGrath he emphasized the importance of quickly reaching dispassionate decisions on who remains on the top team while dealing humanely with the individuals involved: 'Just be completely ruthless in your decisions on people. If you've got your right people in place I think it's very difficult for it *not* to work. Take those decisions quickly and then treat the people decently.'

The appointments that are made and the treatment of those who lose out speak volumes about the new company's business focus and values. A conversation McGrath had with a colleague after the integration illustrates this. McGrath was told that people let go seemed, strangely, not to feel resentful at all. He speculated that this was because these employees perceived the fairness and decency of the process:

It's not always the size of the cheque. It's how people are handled emotionally. You need to explain to them why they lost out – even though they are good and many of them went off to get excellent jobs. I must have seen 100 or 120 people on exit interviews. I cannot tell you how many references I wrote. And I still get Christmas cards from them! Although we were viewed as a fairly rough bunch at Grand Met it was all done in quite a caring way.

Sometimes the media make it difficult for the top team to maintain the merit principle. Journalists interpret senior appointments as a crude signal of which side is winning a perceived power struggle. Rarely if ever will you come across in the business press an interpretation of appointment outcomes that emphasizes merit. Steve Jones, who led the merger of Australia's Metway Bank, Suncorp insurance company and Queensland Investment Development Corporation to form Suncorp-Metway in 1996, recalled how the newspapers were scoring the appointments – almost as if it were a sporting event. In the short run, little can be done to correct such external misperceptions. 'We ignored all that and just kept repeating the message that people were selected on merit. You just have to get through that.'

The 'merit' that is relevant is of course experience and capabilities that are important for the *new* company. That may make some of your appointment decisions difficult for even inside observers to understand – including those directly involved in the appointments process.

Your assessment of how senior managers will perform against future challenges may rest on some highly subjective judgments. Clearly, as much definition as possible about how the new company is to create value will help. So will a detailed, fact-based review of the candidates. Yet in the end you may harbor doubts about some of these calls. Moreover, you are almost certain to regret at least one. CEOs routinely admit as much to us even after highly successful integrations, but often add with a shrug that limited information and decision time make that inevitable.

Alignment on the Top Team

Although appointment decisions can be difficult, at least it is clear to all in the end what you have decided. Top-team alignment, by contrast, is a rather nebulous outcome of many diverse activities. When you *really* have it you will know, but there are various stages along the way when you will ask 'Are we aligned yet?'

In order to secure genuine alignment, as opposed to the superficial variety, many CEOs demand open debate about the company's course. For example, Kevin Sharer of Amgen described how he insisted that each of his eight Executive Committee members take a position on the planned acquisition of

Immunex (which closed in 2002). Amgen's culture fostered independent thinking, but in the end each committee member felt able to declare support for the deal publicly. That support held up throughout the integration process. 'There has never been a minute of recrimination about *whose* deal this is,' Sharer told us. When the new company has been created at the top, senior managers become strongly aligned. It is never my deal or your deal, but always *our* deal.

Achieving such unity on your own side of the merger boundary is difficult enough. Achieving it across the boundary is another level of challenge altogether – particularly under the restricted conditions that apply before the close.

To reach this level, the top team must fashion its own identity *vis-à-vis* the external world of customers, competitors, business partners and regulators. Our survey showed that top teams of merging companies that manage to turn their attention to their external environment often experience a catalytic effect. This carries them past the usual internal frictions much more quickly. In comparison to the pressing need to succeed in the marketplace, these frictions simply do not matter very much. As Michael Kay told us: 'Whenever there were any tensions on the team I would change the subject to customers. They got the message after a while.'

> **A top team finds alignment by turning its attention from itself and the integration to the outside world of customers and competitors.**

This effect is particularly striking when an external crisis suddenly emerges. For example, at one merging company, the integration of the top team had been superficial. After a period of polite behavior, open politicking broke out – a phenomenon that had undermined other mergers in that industry. However, when a financial scandal that seriously threatened the company erupted, the team was finally able to close ranks. A senior manager described the scandal's galvanizing impact:

> It took away all the energy from the turf battles that were starting to build up. The scandal provided a unity within the group that was just unbelievable, and although it cost us dearly, I would say with today's perspective that it was probably one of the best things that could have happened to us. It simply brought the whole thing together. Everybody now knew that there was just no room any more for these internal turf battles.

The external crisis catalyzed the integration of this team. As most top teams will not be so blessed (or cursed?), they must find it in themselves to reach this level of unified external orientation without such help.

In our experience, this is not rocket science. It is mostly a matter of discipline. We often find that the top teams of merging companies establish near-term agendas that are dominated by the 'internal wiring' required by the integration. This is generally unnecessary, particularly if the merging companies have strong integration resources (as many today do).

Every major integration confronts both sets of managers with new customers and business relationships. There is *always* plenty for the newly merged top team to work on here. We will have much more to say about external stakeholders in a later chapter.

In many mergers, some team-building exercises are conducted at the senior level. We generally find that a carefully limited dose of those can be helpful, but there are two important caveats. First, managers on the two sides may have very different perspectives on what is a constructive, businesslike exercise. If one side perceives an activity to be a 'touchy-feely' distraction, it is not worth doing and could be counterproductive. Second, senior managers the world over have very limited patience for time spent on anything other than 'real work'. This is all the more true under the intense pressure of an integration. It is best to focus on outputs whose value is clear, even if intangible (for example, a set of behavioral norms for the new company).

The top team will of course have much real work to do during the integration period, and this can be designed to facilitate its development. However, the design decisions can be tricky. One merging company created a very large steering committee in order to maximize alignment among line managers. The integration manager believed that it did indeed help with that, but it also created a burden for his team. Even retrospectively, there was no consensus among managers as to whether the creation of such a large steering committee was worthwhile.

Role Clarity

The members of the top team share responsibility for the merging company's future as a whole, but they also have distinct individual responsibilities. They must work together in a complementary way not only to succeed with the integration but also to lead the combined company through its other concurrent and future challenges. Ultimately, this requires sharp clarity around roles.

Obviously, this clarity must be reached very quickly for roles directly involved in the integration. The more the integration is driven by the line, the more critical this is. In the case of Diageo, for example, McGrath accelerated the appointments process for this reason: 'We had to put the center together incredibly rapidly because we needed absolute clarity on the people who were going to run the business in each of the functions and below. These people had an awful lot of involvement in the integration.'

From our corporate health perspective, however, with its emphasis on the sustainability of performance over time, the *future* needs of the business are an equally strong factor in defining roles. Creating the new company at the top is as important for the long-term performance of the company as it is for the near-term success of the integration.

> **New senior management roles may be needed to maximize value creation over the long run.**

As we saw in the aborted Alcan–Pechiney–Algroup merger, it was clear that the top team could not even succeed with the integration, not to speak of leading the company in the future. So for the next two integrations Dick Evans and his colleagues at Alcan wanted to make sure that the top team could not only do that but also drive the company forward after the integration. They reached for maximum role clarity in the top team before turning to synergy identification and transition planning. As he explained to us:

> We needed to know where the ownership was. This meant naming the top couple of layers, defining the organizational structure and settling boundary issues, such as which assets go into which business groups. That way there is some certainty as to who is going to own any future action that needs to be taken. We felt that until you have made those decisions it is useless to try to form an integration team.

This captures very well the rationale for creating the new company at the top. Although the top team may be heavily involved in the integration, it is far more than a project team. It carries the responsibility of leading the company in all its endeavors for the indefinite future. It must therefore be set up with this larger responsibility in mind.

The Alcan context was a special one: The aborted three-way merger made it sensible to insist upfront on absolute clarity around managerial accountabilities. In other cases, CEOs have succeeded by insisting on immediate definition of integration responsibilities but deferring clarification of future roles. We observe much variation in practice here, because while any lingering ambiguity around roles has a cost, many CEOs are understandably reluctant to commit themselves while they and their colleagues are in the early stages of learning about each other and about the new company.

In all cases, however, it is important that the top team immediately embodies the new company *as a team* – and that is no small achievement. Effective collaboration around immediate challenges will evolve into clearly demarcated roles soon enough.

What is the 'Top Team'?

You may have noticed that we have not explicitly defined 'top team' in this chapter. Loosely, it means the group of senior managers at the relevant apex that shares general responsibility for the future of their organization. 'Relevant apex' is generally the corporation as a whole, as our discussion generally implies, but may be a group, division or business unit that engages in mergers.

The number of individuals and levels to be counted as part of the top team is therefore highly context-specific. In some cases the top team may be the dozen or fewer people that will interact regularly with the CEO, but for the merger that created JPMorgan Chase in 2001, CEO Bill Harrison told us he appointed 40 people immediately – a flying start that made it possible to move quickly with lower-level appointments as well.

A handful of our interviewees provocatively insisted that the boards of the merging companies be counted as part of the top team. After all, its performance could have a major impact on value creation during the integration and beyond. Thus Don Argus of BHP Billiton pointed to the need to create the new company at board level. His remarks about the boards echo much of what we have said more generally about the top team:

> The role of boards is often underestimated. Very few companies actually change the boards as the result of a merger. But in the same way that the management team needs to be tested for whether it has the right skill set, so should the board be. The capabilities of incumbent directors should be tested and the best chosen. After all, if the board members strike deals among themselves, what signal does this send to the management team? And if the board is polarized, it cannot provide the required leadership and support to the CEO.

Another interviewee noted trenchantly that although standards and processes have been defined over the years for managing the departure of one of the two CEOs (the typical outcome), the integration of boards remains a relatively primitive, largely *ad hoc* process in most companies. Moreover, the boards themselves rarely push for the kind of sensible integration that would result in a streamlined group prepared to support the new company effectively. 'Turkeys don't vote for Christmas.'

Argus, however, said that in his experience if a reasonable process is defined and agreed, it is possible to achieve appropriate board integration. The people you want on the board are obviously those who can most help the new company to create value.

*   *   *

The establishment of the top team poses a critical and immediate challenge for the merging company. The optimal team for the new company's goals must be appointed, and it must be aligned around those goals. Clarity of roles among its members must be achieved for effective collaboration. All this is simply stated and sensible enough, but in practice it can be tough to achieve in the fraught pre-close period – or even soon thereafter.

The four leadership challenges that are discussed in the next four chapters are all secondary to this first one of creating the new company at the top. It takes a strong, cohesive top team to meet the challenges in the areas of the corporate story, culture, external stakeholders and learning. It is nearly impossible, for example, to shape the cultural outcome effectively without a top team that already embodies the desired culture. The new company does indeed start here.

CHAPTER 3

Communicating the Corporate Story

In a 2002 speech, UBS Chairman Marcel Ospel told the highly eventful story of how UBS emerged as a financial giant over the course of a decade. The catalyzing events in this story were a series of acquisitions that culminated in the UBS–SBC merger in 1998.

The story began at SBC. At the start of this period SBC was primarily a collection of Swiss commercial banks (SBC Zurich, SBC Basel, and so on) with a limited international profile, little presence in the capital markets or in institutional asset management, and serious process weaknesses (for example, no segmented reporting or consolidated risk management). Yet it had the aspiration of 'redefining Swiss banking' and becoming a world-class, global financial institution. Ten years later, it had succeeded in the guise of the giant UBS.

M&A was an essential part of this particular story because the aspiration could not have been achieved in the period through organic growth and internal skill development alone. The 1992 acquisition of derivatives house O'Connor & Associates began the series. It was followed by the 1994 acquisition of Brinson Partners, an American institutional asset manager, and the 1995 acquisition of SG Warburg, a British investment bank. One consequence of these acquisitions was that SBC began to run out of excess capital. That contributed to its decision to merge with UBS in 1998. Two years later, the combined entity purchased US stockbroker Paine Webber.

The number and pace of the UBS deals may suggest serial acquisition, but that would be a misinterpretation. Serial acquirers typically do many deals that are highly similar, yet the companies in the UBS story were sharply different in a number of ways. In fact, Ospel insisted that highlighting those differences rather than quickly integrating them away was a major factor in the company's success:

> Almost all these cases contributed a unique set of capabilities,
> resources, franchises or cultural characteristics to our firm.

Emphasizing these distinct contributions, even to the point of exaggerating their impact, creates a sense of immediacy and urgency for a certain transaction and helps to maintain a culture of openness and innovation.

Each round brought the fresh perspectives and talent needed for management renewal. 'In almost all our mergers and acquisitions,' he added, 'very senior leaders joined our top team.'

Companies that embrace such diversity in their M&A programs may face a daunting communications challenge. What the company's strategists may regard as highly synergistic complementarity within a well-defined strategy may appear to outsiders and even to its own managers as a lack of strategic coherence. To these latter observers, the company may seem to be lurching first in one direction and then in another.

As CEO Peter Wuffli explained, however, that was not a problem in the UBS case:

> One success factor is strategic consistency. I think you need a story that makes sense, and we have had a fairly consistent strategy. You lose credibility without it fairly soon, and it can't just be constructed in hindsight: The pieces have to fit so you can explain the deals that you are doing within the framework. In fact, one of our three criteria for a deal was that it has to be strategically obvious – not just explainable, but *obvious*.

Senior managers often wonder why their merger communications efforts falter despite a huge commitment of resources and diligent application of best practices. The surprising answer – at least in many cases – is that the merger has not been *pre*-communicated in the form of a compelling 'corporate story' that enables stakeholder groups to readily understand and commit to it.

Many companies have found that the returns to increasing the intensity of merger communications have become marginal. 'Overcommunicating' even more with each new integration is no longer making much of a difference. The commitment to energetic and sustained communications cannot be faulted, of course, but it is sensible to ask whether we are missing something important here.

> **Years of enhancement of merger communications processes are now yielding marginal returns at many companies.**

A comparison with the top-team challenge is instructive. As we saw in the last chapter, integration of the top team often receives only cursory treatment. In merger communications, however, the opposite is true. Many companies have admirably planned, comprehensive merger communications programs.

Yet the responses to the top-team and merger communications challenges are also similar in a key way: A narrow focus on technical proficiency in performing integration tasks may lead to a dangerous neglect of the larger picture. In the case of the top team, failure to recognize that it is the 'ultimate integration template' may prevent managers from paying sufficient attention to the quality of that template. The new company envisioned in the deal is not created at the top – at least not fully and in a timely way – with consequences all down the line. In the case of merger communications, the need to place the merger within the larger context of the corporate story receives only perfunctory attention at best. The result is that even highly-tuned merger communications fail to deliver the desired impact with managers, employees and other stakeholders.

The Communications Treadmill

These days, the merger communications plans developed by experienced integration teams are impressively thorough and rigorously executed beginning on the day of announcement. Each of the major stakeholder groups – not just employees and investors but also customers, business partners, communities, regulators and others – receives full attention on its own terms. The communications make use of multiple channels and involve every level of management.[1]

Of course, it is not all about mechanics: The message that is conveyed matters as well. There is always the risk that senior managers may (consciously or unconsciously) compromise the communications by not playing straight with stakeholders. For example, the CEOs from both sides in a merger of two professional services firms promised that there would be no layoffs in the partner ranks as a result of the integration. Unfortunately, this seriously strained performance, and they were forced to break the promise the following year. The temptation to create hostages to fortune with such unrealistic promises must of course be resisted.

CEOs may also risk engendering cynicism by describing the merger in positive terms that unnecessarily raise expectations that can be difficult to manage. Lynne Peacock, the integration manager for Barclays Bank's acquisition of the far smaller Woolwich Building Society in the UK in 2000, noted how even the slightest and most casual use of the term 'merger of equals' can create a misleading impression. Even the most sensitively managed and respectful acquisition should not be mislabeled in this way.

So AG Lafley, CEO of Procter & Gamble, emphasized the importance of clarity on this point in connection with P&G's 2005 acquisition of Gillette. Speaking in the early stages of the integration process, he acknowledged the many obvious strengths of Gillette. He noted that it would become a global business unit and a major contributor to innovation in the new company. He expected much two-way learning to take place.

Unfortunately, not all CEOs present a clear picture of how an acquisition will actually work. There is a strong temptation to use vague language about equality, partnership and the like in the beginning and to allow the less pleasant realities of the integration to emerge over time. In our experience, this less than candid approach regularly backfires – as indeed it should.

Many of our interviewees stressed the importance of realism and authenticity. As we saw in the last chapter, an integration may bring moments of truth during which stakeholders' trust in the merging company is on the line. Employees and other stakeholders do not assess the communications in isolation, but rather compare the messages with the realities they observe.

For example, one merging company made a very prominent commitment to conduct the managerial appointments for the top several layers in a rigorous and objective way. Unfortunately, this commitment eroded seriously over time. A senior manager noted that the impact of this failure extended well beyond the management ranks that were directly affected: 'These guys down in the bowels of the organization are smarter than you give them credit for being. They look at this and say, "If these guys fill the management jobs in this way, what does it say about what they really think about *us*?"'

Perhaps most important of all, merger communications have long since moved beyond narrow project efficiency concerns – telling employees what they need to know to achieve the integration process – towards a more interactive approach. Securing support from investors, retaining key managers, and preventing damage to customer relationships are now central objectives in almost every merger communications plan. The best integrators continuously monitor success against such objectives. They also revise communications plans dynamically on the basis of ongoing feedback.

The practical concerns of employees are better understood than a generation ago, and the importance of immediately and directly addressing them is now widely recognized. Steve Kaufman of Arrow Electronics told us that employees 'have three questions: "Will I have a job?" "Who will be my boss?" and "What will my pay point be?" That's all they think about, and until we answer those questions or give them some direction on those questions, there is nothing else on their mind.' Fortunately, it is rare today for a senior manager to open an employee question-and-answer session with a speech about the new company's strategy to people who are worried about losing their jobs.

We agree that too much emphasis on the big picture can be counter-productive, but it is nevertheless important to convey to stakeholders how the merger fits within the larger context. We refer to this context, which stretches in time before and after the merger episode, includes all activities on both sides of the merger boundary, and has specific relevance for each stakeholder group, as the 'corporate story'.

This provides an important clue as to why merger communications are often less than fully successful. Employees and other stakeholders cannot place the merger in context. In effect they cannot *construe* it. They hear the strategic rationale that is offered for the deal, of course, but at a deep level they still do not buy into it because it does not fit well with their understanding of the company and of how they relate to it.

Many communications efforts that remain ineffective do not lack technical proficiency, so continuous refinement of merger communications is not the ultimate answer. The core problem is usually that the corporate story within which the merger takes place has not been effectively communicated *in advance* of the announcement. In the absence of such advance communication, efforts to intensify and refocus merger communications may yield little benefit.

Merging in Context

To business journalists, a merger is a story, and often a very good one. There is plenty of human drama in a major deal, even if it is conducted on friendly terms. Moreover, a few well-placed calls to financial analysts, competitors and customers can yield a rich set of clashing interpretations of the merger. There may also be intriguing speculation on possible countermoves in the industry. In the many cases, however, the merger story disappears from the business pages long before the integration is complete, and indeed often before the deal even closes. Many merger stories do not outlast a single news cycle. As Lynne Peacock told us: 'The merger was big news around here for months, of course, but not in the press. The long articles disappeared soon after the announcement.'

In an ideal world, business journalists would extend their coverage of a merger story right through the last days of the integration. In so doing they would direct attention to the many factors that determine whether the merger is actually creating value. Over time, this would broaden the discussion of how to lead mergers and ultimately make them healthier. Indeed, there appears to be a modest trend in this direction as journalists take up the increasingly probing questions that financial analysts are asking about newly-announced mergers. We also are beginning to see more insightful post-mortem articles a couple years after major mergers.

Telling a Different Story

In any case, senior managers should not allow the urgent need to manage relations with the press during the merger period to narrow their understanding of their own communications role. Their challenge is not simply to communicate the merger story in a richer, more compelling way than journalists, financial analysts and other 'merger storytellers' do. In fact, in a paradoxical way success for corporate leaders actually depends on emphasizing to stakeholders that *the merger is not the story.*

Your challenge is to communicate the merger not actually as a story in itself but rather as an *episode* in a much larger story, one that stretches back into the past of the two companies and forward into their combined future. This corporate story includes not just the merger but also all the company's projects and activities. It is addressed to all of the company's major stakeholders: Customers, employees, business partners, investors and others. This story conveys what the company is, where it is heading, and what this means for every relevant stakeholder group.

> **The merger is never the whole corporate story, but rather just an episode within it.**

We are not introducing a new form of communication here, but simply putting an inclusive label on a large and diverse set of communications that already takes place – more or less effectively – in every company. In your leadership role, you tell your company's story over and over, adjusting the emphasis and format for each audience, and refreshing the details as the company progresses along its path.

The corporate story is not reducible to the strategy, for it includes everything about the company that needs to be told to engage each of its stakeholder groups. For employees, for example, career opportunities and the work culture are important elements of the story. For business partners, terms of the business relationship are paramount. The strategy, then, is a particular version of the story of interest to managers, investors and analysts, that is, those stakeholders who need to focus on how the company will compete.

Crucially, no-one fully controls the story. For each stakeholder the corporate story is not just what they are formally *told by* the company, but also what they *experience of* the company. As Mike Turner, CEO of BAE Systems explained: 'Suppliers, customers, everyone we do business with – they all have a pretty good handle on who we are based on their dealings with us. That's always their starting point, not whatever we have to announce to them.' Thus when the company (then known as British Aerospace) acquired Marconi in 1999, the two companies' business partners had a clear starting point for interpreting the deal.

Your communications can be helpful in framing stakeholder experience, but only if they are consonant with it. Moreover, any variances can hurt. The minor dissonances that can so bedevil your communications in normal times are greatly amplified in a merger integration.

The corporate story is an immense topic, one that includes strategic planning, of course, but also includes areas such as marketing, employee relations, organization development, corporate communications, community relations, investor relations, management development, supply-chain management and much else besides. We will not undertake the vast challenge of outlining how your company becomes what it is for each of its stakeholders. Our purpose here is rather to show that the corporate story provides the inevitable context within which merger communications take place. It is the fact that your story provides such a sprawling context that makes effective merger communications much more than the mechanical challenge that some managers believe it to be.

The Power of the Corporate Story

When a corporate story is clearly and compellingly conveyed, observers need not struggle to see how the latest deal fits in. They understand immediately.

Interestingly, the consistency of the story, particularly in terms of its view of the future, may help to make the company attractive to a range of very different potential partners. As Ospel noted, 'Several of our acquisitions were also very much sought after by other companies – Brinson Partners, for example, and Paine Webber. An attractive long term vision was a central element of success in convincing the leaders of these firms.' The story makes it easier to execute a series of sharply contrasting, opportunistic deals provided that the story makes each of them 'strategically obvious'. In general, the more clearly your story has been conveyed, the easier it will be for stakeholders of all kinds to understand how a string of superficially disparate deals fits within it.

All too often the merger announcement hits stakeholders as a bolt from the blue – a sudden, disconcerting event that they struggle to understand. The resulting confusion may completely blindside a CEO, as one confessed to us:

> The market reaction was much more negative than I ever thought it could be. It was not expressed in stock price as much as in the voices of the analysts and investors. 'Last month, you had a great story, and then, just three weeks later, you announced this acquisition and injected new uncertainties. What do you need this for?' So the whole strategic rationale – where we thought we had a very compelling case – turned out to be less embraced than I would have wished.

Like any other CEO in this position, this one engaged in a flurry of explanatory communications to analysts and investors. This cost him time that was even more scarce than usual due to the demands of the integration. It also compounded the internal communications challenge as managers and employees on both sides of the merger boundary were influenced by the external skepticism.

So the inability of stakeholders to place your merger in context can have serious consequences. Ideally, therefore, the story should *already* be so strongly embedded among all relevant stakeholder groups that they automatically interpret the merger in its terms.

> **Effective communication of the corporate story before the merger is announced is ideal, because that would enable stakeholders to interpret the merger themselves.**

When effective pre-communication of the story has been achieved, the communications work for the merger itself is already half done at the point of announcement. The corporate story already contains the rationale for the merger – and indeed for any other major initiative that the company undertakes. The answer to the question 'Why do this merger?' is simply that it drives the company's story forward. If it does not, you should not be doing the deal. If it does, your chances for a successful integration are higher even if the deal itself was opportunistic rather than anticipated in your strategic plans.

The corporate story – the codification of the 'why' – takes time to communicate, and typically requires much discussion before it truly sinks in.

We find that it may take new CEOs a couple of years to refashion the corporate story they have inherited and to convey it to stakeholders. By contrast, what needs to be communicated at the time of announcement is the 'what' and the 'how' of the merger – and these points, however unpalatable some of them may be, are conceptually much more straightforward and easier to understand.

Moreover, the 'what' and the 'how' flow naturally from the 'why'. For example, if a company's story involves the development of new capabilities, and an acquisition is undertaken to gain critical skills, then it is clear that the integration must be conducted in a way that preserves those skills. Concretely, this will involve a heavy talent retention effort and perhaps an effort to shelter parts of the acquired company from the parent's influence. It may also require, in fact, a keen concern for learning about the intangible strengths of the acquired company as the project progresses so that the integration can be dynamically adjusted to protect those strengths. In any case, if the 'why' is clear, managers and employees can readily understand the rest.

> **The 'why' of the corporate story goes a long way to making the 'what' and the 'how' of merger communications clear and compelling.**

The unfortunate reality today is that many merger announcements are loaded down with a double communications burden: The struggle to convey the practical details of the merger, as well as the larger corporate story within which the merger is supposed to make sense. You may face this double burden even if you have made real effort to communicate the story in advance. You may wrongly suppose that your story is well embedded with relevant stakeholder groups. As we saw in the case of the CEO that was blindsided by resistance from analysts and investors, the fit between the merger and the story that may be obvious to you may escape them entirely.

Thus however much we insist that the story should be pre-communicated, we recognize that this does not always work fully. You should strive to ensure that deals are strategically obvious, but cannot count on them always being so.

Communicating both the story and the merger simultaneously need not be an insuperable problem, but it requires engagement of people at two very different levels. Getting the balance between them right is key. To err on one side is to present the story in an abstract way that does not connect to employees and others that have immediate and practical concerns. The other extreme is to focus so much on the nuts and bolts of the merger that employees and others cannot place it in its context, that is, they cannot see the 'why'.

An imbalance in either direction can have the same de-energizing result: People feel like cogs in a soulless machine. The integration ordeal has no apparent meaning for them, no purpose. The middle way involves continuous movement between the merger and the broader story it helps to enact. Ultimately, *your* challenge – as opposed, say, to that of HR and external relations people on the integration team – is to place the merger communications within the context of the corporate story.

The Role of the 'Backstory'

CEOs naturally and appropriately emphasize the future in merger communications, but the old saying 'you can't get there from here' may apply. Stakeholders' sense of what is possible for the company's future course is strongly influenced by the 'backstory', that is, the past events in the company's history that continue to affect their thoughts and behavior.[2] If you respect the influence of the backstory you may be able to lead the integration in a way that builds upon it rather than conflicts with it.

However, some CEOs speak and act as if the merger provides a clean-slate opportunity to start the corporate story all over again from the present moment. The newly-merged company, they claim, has no history. The integration, it seems, involves the *dis*-integration of the past. Yet in reality no leader can move a merging company to a new and perhaps very different future without taking seriously the powerful influences of the backstory.

> **There are no clean slate mergers. For better or worse, the 'backstory' always matters.**

For example, a large industrial company had experimented for a number of years with an organizational design that was intended to overcome the problem of functional silos. Both structure and processes were redesigned to promote cross-functional collaboration. Unfortunately, the organization resisted the new emphasis, and after the CEO who had introduced it departed, his successor reinstated the familiar functional organization.

Managers and employees have remarkable memories for discarded organizational experiments. The failure of the cross-functional organization was therefore a highly relevant element of this company's backstory. Any attempt to work cross-functionally during the integration or in the new company could be expected to face resistance. And that in fact is what happened. The resistance was not recognized in time, and those integration initiatives that depended upon cross-functional collaboration were largely unsuccessful. Managers and employees were always quick to say: 'We tried that before and it just doesn't work.'

What could the new CEO have done? Most obviously he could have strongly communicated to relevant managers that the return of the functional organization was no excuse for failing to collaborate cross-functionally during the integration. He also could have structured the work of the integration in a way that might overcome the problems of the past. For example, if one of the problems in the old organization was that functional heads simply could not reach agreement after months of wrangling, he could have played a tiebreaker role during the integration.

The backstory is not, of course, only a negative legacy. Michael Kay, the former CEO of Sky Chefs, found that his organization's successful turnaround provided it with great transformational energy. A few years later that energy contributed substantially to the success of the company's integration of Caterair.

Kay had led the company through a major performance turnaround program in the early 1990s. This led to a bold, 'can do' story within the company – the perfect ground for the 1995 acquisition of Caterair. Someone once asked Kay what might have happened if the industry had not been ripe for consolidation in the mid-1990s. Where would all the momentum from the turnaround have gone? He replied: 'We would have found something else that would have continued to propel us forward in huge steps. We had created this massive appetite among the managers, the employees and the shareholders. There was no putting the beast back in its cage.'

After the deal the beast was still on the prowl, but the focus for performance improvement turned inwards. Sky Chefs launched a major procurement initiative and adopted lean techniques from the manufacturing sector. Kay insists that the company expected regular rounds of major change: 'We had created a culture that needed to be fuelled on a continuing basis. We didn't say "We met the post-merger expectation, so now let's just run the business." '

Note the sequence here: First a turnaround, then a large merger, then additional performance improvement initiatives, with the entire sequence constituting Sky Chefs' transformational corporate story in the 1990s. Very frequently the merger is *not* the first major episode in such a story, and even when it is, the story should be well communicated to stakeholder groups in advance for reasons that we have outlined earlier in this chapter.

The Momentum Trap

It takes miles to change the course of an ocean liner moving at full speed. The momentum imparted by a powerful corporate story has a similar effect, as stakeholders tend to project its backstory into the future.

Just as managers may almost demand the continuation of a corporate story that energizes them, other stakeholders might be slow to recognize an important change in your corporate story, however insistently you communicate it to them. For example, if you have executed a number of mergers in rapid sequence, business journalists and financial analysts may continue to speculate on your next deal even after you have clearly signaled that you are switching to organic growth. This may make the switch more difficult.

We asked Peter Wuffli whether it would be difficult to transfer the focus to organic growth. He replied: 'Yes, absolutely, that's my biggest challenge right now. And you see it in the press, which doesn't want to believe us. That's why every three months they write articles about how we are talking to everybody about deals.'

Interestingly, although the press may not want to believe you, they will nevertheless hold you responsible for what you tell them. That was the experience of a European CEO that announced a switch to organic growth but then surprised the markets and the press with a major merger. The loss of credibility drew as much attention as the merger itself.

Part of the challenge in changing direction is simply making stakeholders aware of the switch, part is convincing them that you can succeed with it, and part, of course, is actually succeeding. As Wuffli commented, 'We are very good at acquiring and integrating, but we are not yet as good at dealing with organic growth. It requires patience and the redeployment of management, and you need different financial instruments to measure your progress. It's just a different mode of operation.'

For stakeholder groups, including your own managers, success breeds expectations of the *same kind* of success. The audiences for your corporate story are naturally conservative. As we saw in the case of the blindsided CEO earlier in this chapter, they will require much convincing if you wish to change a corporate story that seems to them to be working well enough.

Managing the Backstory

However much you may want to focus your storytelling on the future of the combined company, employees and other stakeholders will naturally make sense of it in terms of what they know best: The backstory. Does the merger signal a break with the backstory? Or does it mark a continuation of it? At a more granular level, what will change and what will stay the same?

In communicating the corporate story, therefore, you should not try to wipe the slate clean. Instead, you should start where your audiences are. For example, a merger might signal a continuation of a company's story about achieving scale through rolling up competitors in the industry. But at the same time, there may be some capabilities in the target that could provide a platform for important new ventures. This is actually a common pattern in mergers: Relative continuity at the corporate level is combined with major change with a specific business area. It is important that stakeholders identify clearly both those respects in which the story continues on as before and those in which there is a significant change.

> **Stakeholders need to be able to see in what ways the merger signals a 'momentum story', and in what ways it signals a 'breakaway story'.**

Consider, for example, the sequence of four banking mergers that started with Chemical Bank's merger with Manufacturers Hanover in 1991. There followed mergers with Chase Manhattan Bank in 1996, with JP Morgan in 2001 and with Bank One in 2004. As these were all major deals that pushed JPMorgan Chase towards its strategic objective of much greater scale, one simple interpretation is that the bank started with a breakaway story in the early 1990s which shifted towards a momentum story as the second, third and fourth increments in scale came 5, 10 and 13 years later, respectively. Yet with the JP Morgan merger the bank moved strongly into investment banking, and with the recent Bank One merger it is establishing major retail operations outside the New York City area for the first time.

There is not much point in debating whether with these last two deals the bank has moved back to a breakaway story or not. It is critical, however, for investors, employees and other stakeholders to recognize in what particular ways the story is changing over time, and in what ways it is not. The major moves into investment banking and the geographic expansion of retail banking are indeed new moves, but they are set against the background of continuing momentum towards greater scale.

In sum, the influence of the backstory can take many forms, positive and negative. In general, the backstory has a conservative effect on the company, reinforcing any momentum that is there but impeding any major change of direction. This explains why the shock of a major merger sometimes has surprisingly little effect on the company's trajectory – at least immediately. The merger might be readily interpreted as confirmation of its backstory. The response is not 'this too shall pass' but rather 'this is just more of the same.'

The total long-term impact of a merger – its 'health' in our terms – depends in subtle ways on how effectively you guide such interpretations among stakeholders. For example, you might intend to use small acquisitions to change the culture and capabilities of the parent in far-reaching ways. As we saw in the UBS case, this is indeed possible. Yet as Ospel underscored, it requires that these valuable features of the acquisition receive regular, heavy emphasis 'even to the point of exaggerating their impact'.

*   *   *

Communications is not just about delivering messages, but also about connecting with people in ways that are relevant to them and that trigger positive responses. Experts in communication have delivered *that* message for many years.

The greatest challenge here is making the imaginative leap that enables you to understand deeply the whole network of people – employees and many others – on whom your merger's health depends. This will always be hard work and claim a major share of senior management time. The concept of the corporate story can be helpful here – not least because it makes it so difficult to slide into the lazy habit of reducing communications to delivering messages.

CHAPTER 4

Establishing a New Performance Culture

'Hey, you know, I'm probably your worst damn nightmare. The evil empire to the south shows up in charge here and it's somebody from L.A. I mean, if only we could have been from Boston. *Any place but L.A.*' Kevin Sharer, CEO of California-based biotech giant Amgen, is in Seattle joking with employees of its 2002 acquisition Immunex. Yet melding together the two corporate cultures was no laughing matter.

Sharer said that Amgen's integration of Synergen back in 1994 was 'an unmitigated disaster that turned out to be an important how-not-to-do-it experience that informed my thinking' for the Immunex deal eight years later. The earlier acquisition paid off economically because a sleeper drug turned out to be a big hit, but the integration was much more chaotic and painful for all concerned than it needed to be. Sharer was determined not to repeat that experience.

So, shortly after the Immunex announcement he invited the few Synergen managers who had stayed with Amgen to a special set of meetings. There they re-played the experience of being acquired by Amgen. This enabled Sharer to understand what it is like to be on the target's side, and he used this understanding to raise the sensitivity of his own managers. 'I frequently sat our people down and said, "You need to understand what it's like when you're talking with those people in Immunex. Imagine if a pharma giant bought us and you were listening to the guys from there. Think of how you'd feel! Because, as far as the guys from Immunex are concerned, we *are* a pharma giant."'

This level of sympathetic imagination towards an acquisition was rare not so long ago. Nowadays many acquirers aspire to achieve it, though few go to the lengths to which Amgen did. Intense integration pressures make it difficult to find the time and mental space to learn about a merger partner in more than a superficial way. For all that, we are heartened to witness an ever greater determination to do so in many companies. This is an extremely healthy trend.[1]

Faced with these cultural challenges, managers increasingly recognize the importance of what one might call 'corporate character': The patience, openness and humility required to learn about another company's strengths, a willingness to compromise to preserve those strengths, authentic concern for how people on the other side are experiencing the integration, and resistance of the temptation to mask unpleasant issues with 'feel good' rhetoric. All these qualities require that a basic level of fundamental human decency remain active throughout the trials of the integration period.

A large majority of senior managers (and presumably of our readers) consider the effective management of culture a critical factor in integration success. There might remain a few holdouts, but it would take us too far afield to make the case for culture's importance here. We will therefore take this as read.

However, this does not actually simplify the challenge of addressing this topic very much. General agreement on culture's importance has not led to comparable agreement on what to do about it, and actual practice around what is loosely called 'cultural integration' differs very markedly.

> **Almost every manager affirms the pivotal importance of culture in mergers, but the agreement ends there.**

The key here is to focus on establishing the 'performance culture', that is, the subset of cultural features that are most relevant for how the new company will create value. After all, the success of the merger ultimately depends upon the ways in which managers and employees in the merged company collaborate in value creation.

You could fail to establish this performance culture by doing either too little or too much. If you take a radical hands-off approach to culture, you risk the emergence of a new company that lacks the energy and discipline needed to create value as envisioned. You may even find that the merged company is in some ways culturally weaker than either predecessor company. The opposite extreme of trying to achieve comprehensive cultural integration within the integration period is also flawed. That approach could so overburden your project that critical business goals such as the retention of customers and the smooth operation of your core processes may be compromised. Paradoxically, such a heightened level of attention to culture could also backfire by sparking cultural conflict between the two sides.

Although focusing on the performance culture seems straightforward, in reality this can be very challenging even for managers that are 'culturally musical'. For example, we have found that many senior managers are very articulate about the effect that culture has on corporate performance. Often they can acutely diagnose both the positive and the negative effects of a given cultural trait. Yet even many of these managers unconsciously hold untenable views about the prospects for changing culture in positive ways. They suppose it to be more malleable that it actually is.

In particular, the adoption of either of the two widely-held cultural myths that we will discuss in this chapter can have an insidious effect. Managers who cling to either the *survival of the fittest myth* or the *cultural integration myth* may adopt a highly ineffective approach to dealing with culture during an integration. Therefore, after a quick overview of a few points of wide agreement that are clearly sound we will turn to a detailed consideration of the two cultural myths. Once these have been cleared away it will be possible to define a robust approach for establishing the performance culture that is key to the health of any merger. In order to link culture to value, we need to frame those issues very carefully.

Culture: A Point of Departure

Academic research into the complex topic of culture in a merger context has yielded tentative and sometimes even contradictory findings.[2] Nevertheless, in recent years we have witnessed three clear advances among sophisticated integrators in their management of culture. Sophisticated integrators (1) identify strategic risks related to culture, (2) rigorously diagnose relative cultural strengths and (3) factor culture into their integration planning. Each of these actions requires some elaboration.

It is clear that strategically important cultural features could be at risk during an integration. Such features could lie on either side of the merger boundary, but most attention is typically paid to the more vulnerable of the two parties. Extensive coverage of acquisition fiascos in the business press partly accounts for this concern with the vulnerable. In these disasters the acquirer is blamed for stifling the entrepreneurialism or innovativeness of what it has acquired. The dominant company comes across as the bureaucratic, arrogant partner that destroyed what it bought. Such stories have been told so often over the last couple of decades that even managers with no merger experience at all sense the dangers when they read about a giant acquiring a high-performing small company.

Increasingly, however, managers are recognizing that mergers of equals also may involve serious strategic risks related to culture. In these cases, it is now widely agreed that either side may be culturally stronger in key areas. As Orange's Jean-François Pontal put it: 'My starting assumption is always that there may be something in the other side's culture that could make us stronger. If you don't start with such an assumption, you will never take the trouble to look.' Therefore an attempt is usually made to identify and capture the complementary strengths of the two sides.

Of course the other possibility – that one side's culture could be objectively superior in most or all business-relevant dimensions – is also a real one that executives with their responsibilities to shareholders should not overlook, notwithstanding its lack of political correctness. Indeed, the fast-paced roll-up acquisition programs of some successful serial acquirers are based on this hard-nosed perspective. So strictly speaking the diagnosis of relative cultural strengths is not always important, but in this book we focus on mergers of equals and large acquisitions where it generally is.

There are also a few cases where the weaker of the two companies actually has several top executives who are better champions of the newly merged company's culture than their counterparts are. In one case, a CEO acquired the company that he had led a few years earlier. He reasoned that he needed its more performance-oriented management culture and despaired of instilling it incrementally in his current company.

These two advances – the discovery that culture can make a difference strategically and the recognition that either side may possess valuable cultural strengths – lead naturally enough to a third: The determination to factor culture into integration planning.

In general, the need to preserve important cultural features may compel managers to adopt a more conservative integration scope. In fact, cultural considerations can feed back all the way to the negotiations stage. Steve Kaufman of Arrow Electronics, for example, said he was willing to pay more for a company when he knew that the cultural integration challenge was not going to be difficult. Similarly, Bill Harrison, the CEO of JPMorgan Chase who over a decade went through three huge mergers of equals between New York banks, told us about making sure each time that there was a 'range of manageability of cultural differences'. These differences can be exploited to build a stronger company. This was also the experience of Thorlief Krarup, who was formerly the Group CEO of Nordea (the current name, adopted in 2001, for the bank that emerged from a series of Scandanavian bank mergers). 'We need to believe', he told us, 'that cultural differences can have a positive impact, and that open-mindedness towards these differences will over time create enormous synergy and energy.' So it is not surprising that companies with strong merger experience include in their integration planning both the risks and the opportunities entailed in any cultural differences found.

Unfortunately, there is no consensus on *how* to do this. Some companies take a *laissez-faire* approach to culture on the assumption that a desirable cultural outcome will emerge naturally through the intensive interaction of the two sides. At the other end of the spectrum, other companies adopt a strongly interventionist approach. They develop elaborate cultural integration programs that involve extensive, explicit discussion of culture in cascading workshops. Most companies fall somewhere between these extremes of benign neglect and aggressive interventionism.

> **In the absence of any consensus on what to do, corporate leaders adopt a range of approaches for influencing the culture of merging companies.**

We believe that choices along this spectrum are affected by leaders' often-unconscious acceptance of one of two popular myths about culture in mergers. Acceptance of either tends to lead to a poor outcome. Both cause managers to take a predetermined approach to culture rather than working out what is needed for the concrete case at hand.

The Cultural Myths

Two common myths about culture seem to retain an unconscious hold on many managers. The *survival of the fittest myth* posits a natural process of cultural engagement in which the superior culture automatically triumphs. The *cultural integration myth* supposedly frees you from the need to worry about the merging company's culture. According to the latter, culture is malleable stuff that you can reshape at will during the hectic integration period. Thus the cultures of the two predecessor companies impose scarcely any constraints on you at all. Fortunately, it is relatively easy to dispel both myths once they have been explicitly described. Neither can stand up to close scrutiny.

The Survival of the Fittest Myth

Acquirers that buy poorer-performing companies seem to be particularly captivated by the survival of the fittest myth. The CEO of a European bank argued that since the superiority of the acquirer's culture was acknowledged by the target's managers, there could be no doubt about which culture would prevail. Therefore no concrete steps would need to be taken to address the target's cultural weaknesses.

It may be reasonable for an acquirer to assume that its target's weaker culture could not possibly prevail over its own – particularly if the target is much smaller. However, it is *not* reasonable to assume that a weaker culture at the target is fated to disappear. Although in general buying poorer-performing companies to improve them is a better bet than buying better-performing companies to be improved *by them*, it is not a sure bet. The less fit culture might survive alongside the fitter culture for years. Indeed, this is actually a common outcome. Therefore successful serial acquirers that follow roll-up strategies to improve their targets' performance (such as GE Capital) do not ascribe to the survival of the fittest myth. They make very sure their superior culture is *imposed* on the target in a very disciplined and systematic way.[3]

For mergers of equals, the situation is more complex. Since neither side has the natural dominance of an acquirer that is many times the size of its acquisition both cultures are effectively 'in play'. Either might prevail in the end. Moreover, ending up with the worst possible mix of the two is a real possibility. To see why this is so, we need to look closely at how two cultures interact during a merger – and in particular at the ways in which the ultimate survivor is actually 'fittest'.

We have seen cases where the fittest competitor in the *internal* competition of a merger is the company that has the best survival traits for the artificial pressure-cooker environment of an integration. These might not necessarily be what the combined company needs to prevail in the *external* competition of the marketplace after the integration is complete. So the survival of the fittest (in one sense) leaves the merged company less fit (in another sense).

> **Those who imagine that the 'fitter' corporate culture will automatically prevail need to ask themselves: Fit for what?**

For example, during an integration, the more hard-edged, numbers-oriented, individualistic culture may indeed run rings around a more innovative and collaborative culture that places high value on building long-term capabilities and strengthening customer relationships. In these circumstances, the hard currency of short-term, quantifiable results tends to be valued more highly than intangible options on the future. (The situation is analogous to placing an alligator and a dolphin together in a tank. As a species, the dolphin has evolved far further in terms of intelligence, but it would not survive the encounter.)

A major part of the rationale for a merger between two professional services firms was that the collaborativeness and global outlook of what we could call the 'options' firm could be extended to the 'hard currency' firm. Strategically, this made sense because clients were demanding services that could only be provided by the first kind of firm.

To respond to these demands, the 'options' firm had developed an elaborate set of systems and processes, and it was not always immediately evident who was contributing the most to its complex requirements. In the other firm, it was much easier to keep score because the intangible contributions just did not count. A former partner of the 'options' firm explained: 'You can imagine a local manager from the hard-edged firm saying to his counterpart, "What are your numbers?" And the other guy would respond, "Well, the numbers are a bit down this month but that's because we've helped a team in Singapore." But that just doesn't cut much ice with someone who doesn't care about that.' During an integration a surprising number of people may stop caring about such things, at least temporarily.

British Aerospace's 'Benchmark' culture-change program had run for several years leading up to the 1999 acquisition of Marconi Electronic Systems. This program involved all levels of the organization. The Chairman, Sir Richard Evans, noted with satisfaction that the Marconi managers were immediately won over by the British Aerospace culture: 'From what I've heard from other people, there is a very strong feeling that the British Aerospace values were pretty firmly embedded, and the Marconi managers looked at them and said, "Well, we want those. That's the kind of culture we want to operate in, and you guys have already got it, so that's fine."'

During the integration, however, some important 'soft' aspects of the Benchmark program fell by the wayside, while the performance orientation of the Marconi people gained ground. Evans' original intention had been to suspend Benchmark during the integration and revive it afterwards, but the program was never restarted. Although Sir Richard considered the merger as a whole a success, he concedes that the outcome could have been better yet if Benchmark had contributed more: 'I think one of the key ingredients would have been to manage people better. Out of almost desperation to succeed, we reverted to type. I think if we had been another two years into the Benchmark program, we'd have been able to protect the values better.'

Yet Mike Turner, the current CEO, shed no tears over the program:

> With the Benchmark program I think we'd become a bit soft. It was a sideshow in a way, something apart from the real business. And the problem was it was also creating things to do that, in my view, were interfering with the real business.
>
> Marconi already was performance-driven. So I think the two have come together at a good time. Now the focus really is on performance. Yes, we're going to look after our people, and yes, clearly the customer is important. And we have to keep innovating, but we also have got to perform. It's quite tough out there.

Evans and Turner agree that in some sense the Marconi culture 'won' the internal competition even though the competition was 'fixed' by managers on both sides in favor of the British Aerospace culture. Turner argues, however, that *external* competition was driving British Aerospace in Marconi's direction anyway. Turner even insisted that winding down the cultural change program could be seen as a healthy by-product of the merger. Evans of course disagrees.

There is no way to settle this debate. The case does clearly show, however, that one cannot simply count on the 'fittest' of the two cultures prevailing in an integration process where even the definition of 'fit' may be contested.

The Cultural Integration Myth

What is an employee's experience when his or her company is taken over by a much larger one and loses its identity? Kevin Sharer comes right to the point: 'Those people feel like they have been conquered. It doesn't matter how you sugarcoat it – you know, "It's a merger of equals," "Gee, you're a great company, and we're a great company." The fact is that Immunex's name disappears, and that's just bloody awful.'

Why is it so awful? Why is it so difficult to adopt the norms of a new culture, or to find a mutually acceptable compromise between one's own culture and another? If this problem seems exaggerated to us, it might be because we tend to think of culture first and foremost in terms of a few superficial stylistic variances between different nationalities. So the Japanese are polite, the Germans are orderly, the Americans are casual, and so on. However, when two companies come together, what they find is a seemingly endless range of deeply-rooted cultural differences that have practical implications for how business gets conducted – or *not* conducted.

One difference that becomes starkly obvious in many integrations is that between corporate paternalism and individual accountability. At what point does pressure put on managers to perform cause dysfunctional behaviors that outweigh the advantages of strong focus and discipline? In almost every industry one can find two successful companies that have answered this question very differently. When they come together the right setting for the combined company is an open question, one that depends in particular on their strategies.

Again, one company may insist on finality and clarity in decision-making, while the other prefers to allow decisions to be reopened to take account of any new facts and ideas. Alistair Imrie noted this cultural difference during the BAE Systems integration:

> They had a management culture in Marconi where, when they made up their minds to do something, they all did it. In British Aerospace we had a process where we thought we had made up our minds to do something, but the process had sufficient ambiguity that a proportion of people would not feel bound to observe that line, and to some extent or another would feel that they had the freedom to either depart from it slightly or, in some cases, significantly.

It does not take much imagination to picture how tenaciously the two sides of an integration might cling to their familiar decision-making rules and routines – or their rules for making a business case.

John McGrath exaggerates a little to point up the contrast he saw at Diageo's predecessor companies: 'Here's two caricatures: Grand Met management were hip shooters in a data-free zone and Guinness was a case of analysis paralysis, but if they do buy anything they'll wind up paying twice as much as we would. Neither is entirely accurate but there's a grain of truth in both.' There are a host of opportunities for the two sides to lock horns over such differences. For example, one side may see much more work ahead in estimating synergies, while the other might be impatient to drop the analysis and move on.

Even differences in the *format* of a business case can be a stumbling block. When GE Medical Systems and Amersham plc combined in 2004 to form GE Healthcare, GE managers found that the managers of their high-performing acquisition used text memos for written business communications – a format that the Powerpoint presentation had supplanted at GE long ago. For a time, both sides found the other side's preference exasperating.

Another cultural variable that comes into play in almost every integration is the location of decision-making. In every decentralized company there is some tension between the corporate center and the field over key decision-making authority. Most companies find some reasonable compromise that both sides can live with, and tinker with it from time to time. However, when two companies come together, they normally find that they have reached different compromises. Although the importance of these differences might not register at all in the CEO's thinking, they could be extremely important for pivotal employees far removed from headquarters. Steve Kaufman offers a gritty example:

> Say we buy a company where the salesmen rule, where no order is a bad order, where they say 'yes' to every customer and supplier and assume people in the back room will somehow make it work. When we start to impose our set of standards, some of their sales people will feel very constricted. You hear things like: 'Some clerk back at corporate can overrule me? What kind of bull is that? I'm a general manager.'

In the salespeople's minds, that lost authority might outweigh other supposedly more 'practical' benefits offered by the acquirer, such as a better commission schedule and a more competitive product line. Widespread losses of field personnel can be precipitated by seemingly small differences in the corporate philosophies around central control versus local autonomy. If you focus only on the impact of 'big' decisions to shut down factories or close product lines, you might take a surprise hit to your revenue line.

In cross-border mergers these problems may be compounded by communication failures. Jean-François Pontal, the former CEO of Orange, told us how an implicit English 'no' can be translated into an explicit French 'yes':

> As you know, the French are very good at improvisation: There's a situation, they get an idea, and then they just improvise a lot. In the beginning when the UK guys saw where the French were heading, they said 'That's very interesting. We should think about that.' They didn't just say 'No'. So the French thought they had agreed, and at the last moment they ran into problems because the UK guys were very upset.

Pontal concluded that 'the main effect of national cultural differences is that *people think they understand each other when they do not*'. A working knowledge of the other side's national language is not enough to bridge this chasm. This problem, of course, is familiar to any manager with international experience. Under the pressure-cooker conditions of an integration, however, the temptation to proclaim that cross-cultural understanding has been achieved when it is still superficial may become acute.

It is easy to fall into the view that the way they do things at a competitor in the same industry – perhaps headquartered in the same city – is not likely to be so starkly different from yours. You might think 'They're in life insurance like us, and I run into these guys at conferences all the time. I know what they're like, so if we buy them it'll be an easy integration.'

Yet that is where the trap lies. How many salespeople, for example, will jump ship before the acquiring insurer discovers that its rules for clawing back commissions cross one of their 'red lines'? Hans-Gert Penzel, who led the 1998 integration that created Germany's Bayerische Hypotheken und Vereinsbank (now HVB Group), recounted how the managers in the headquarters of the two Bavarian banks – just two kilometers apart – underestimated the culture differences between them. 'The next time', he added, 'we would do a cultural due diligence in order to understand better the ways in which the two are different.'

Cultural variations are far too pervasive and intangible, and are too deeply rooted in shared experience of the two companies, to be engineered away in the cultural integration workstream of an integration project. The cultural integration myth – the belief that such engineering is possible – is reinforced by the lax habit of seeing culture in grand but superficial terms. We need instead to recognize the numerous small but telling differences that find expression in processes like business decision-making, performance measurement, and personnel evaluation.

> **Cultural differences are far too pervasive and subtle for immediate and comprehensive cultural integration to be feasible.**

We are not, however, offering a counsel of despair. Companies can live with many lingering cultural differences from their predecessor companies. Indeed, these differences can sometimes add productive diversity in team settings. As Marcel Ospel of UBS argued in the last chapter, the explicit celebration of cultural differences can have a powerfully positive effect on a company's competitiveness by making it more dynamic and flexible.

At a more mundane level, many companies perform very well despite a high degree of cultural variation between functional areas or between regions. No one has argued that all these cultural differences must be eliminated, so why should we assume that cultural variation introduced through a merger is always harmful?

Moreover, as a practical matter, in many integrations a large percentage of the employees will continue to work in their current locations largely with colleagues from the same predecessor company. Any serious cultural issues to be dealt with are often confined largely to the senior managerial ranks and to a relative handful of points of interface between the two operations. Indeed, some of those deals that business journalists say fail due to 'widespread corporate culture clashes' are actually the victims of ego conflicts at senior levels.

Yet in our view persistent cultural differences in critical areas – for example, over when a decision is final – account for much of the excess attrition that is often observed months or even years after the integration project ends. After all, the outcomes of the competition between these different ways of working largely define what it means to be an effective contributor to the company. Is the manager who calls for further analysis of a problem adding value? The answers to questions like that may determine which managers thrive in the new company.

Beyond Cultural Integration

The histories of the two cultural myths differ. The survival of the fittest myth seems to be fading, to judge from the number of managers who explicitly advocate it, and there is thus an emerging consensus in favor of some form of cultural intervention. However, in our view this consensus is unduly colored by the second myth that suggests culture can be readily reshaped. Indeed, some managers think of it almost as a technical problem. If product lines, business processes, retail networks and IT systems can be fully integrated, why not the two cultures in the same way?

This reasoning overlooks the scale and complexity of the challenge: It would be hubris to suppose that one can readily effect whatever cultural change one desires across two merging companies, each of which may have tens of thousands of employees in scores of countries and a dozen or more distinct professional subcultures.

Nor is it clear that such a uniform global culture would be desirable, at least in some industries. Lars Norby, the CEO of Group 4 Securicor, saw this clearly as he reflected on his sprawling worldwide organization with 300,000 employees in almost 90 countries: 'Superimposing one general "McDonald's" culture worldwide just wouldn't work. Not in a business like this one. We operate in countries with major cultural differences. From a commercial point of view, sensitivity to those national cultures is much more important than a common corporate culture.'

This argument for immediate and comprehensive cultural integration is also flawed because it compares culture, which largely emerges through human interactions over an extended period, with the artifacts of human design like IT systems. So even if extensive cultural integration is desirable, it cannot be achieved overnight. Leaders need to consider what they can do to promote and guide this cultural emergence from human interactions, during and long after the integration.

The Role of the Performance Contract

The healthiest outcome of a merger can be achieved by focusing attention on the *performance culture* needed for the new company. By this we mean the relatively small set of mindsets and behaviors that are crucial to establish the merged company in a promising path for the future. The limited amount of change needed to establish a pattern of success *in terms of value creation* will then in turn foster the emergence of a broader range of mindsets and behaviors among a wider set of corporate actors.

This requires a sharp focus. The objective is not to identify and reconcile every conceivable us-versus-them cultural contrast between the two companies. That could lead to a preoccupation with pre-merger corporate identities or even to a form of cultural horse-trading ('We'll accept your approach to business decision-making as long as you accept our set of people values').

The emphasis should be squarely on what is needed to be successful in the future, and the more concrete, externally-oriented and business-like the description of this is, the better. A merged company that is succeeding in the marketplace will evolve naturally in ways that build on that success. Your challenge during the integration is to create the cultural conditions for it, not to pursue the corporate-culture equivalent of utopia through a far-reaching cultural integration effort.

At the heart of the performance culture is the *performance contract*. This is the set of mutual obligations that enables both sides to create a new company that can meet its performance potential. Such a contract consists of standards for running the business: How you serve customers, how you manage processes, what quality levels are to be reached, how you interact with colleagues, how you make decisions and much else are laid out in more or less explicit form. The new performance contract at Diageo, for example, mandated the widespread use of value-based management, a performance management approach that McGrath said changed the culture on the Guinness side much more than classic cultural change tools like values statements.

> **Establishment of a powerful performance culture depends upon the definition of a 'performance contract' that spells out mutual obligations in the new company.**

Every company has at least an implicit performance contract, although its quality may be poor. A merger provides an opportunity to reinforce or revise the performance contract.

When managers of an acquired company must adapt to the ways of a new parent, it is particularly important that the new performance contract be fully explained early on. Dick Evans recalled that Alcan's managers fell short in this regard for the 2000 Algroup acquisition, so for the 2004 Pechiney acquisition they were much more thorough: 'We had learned from the Algroup integration the importance of laying out clear guidelines and expectations at the very beginning so that the Pechiney people would know how to behave, because they would be looking for those signals.'

The effectiveness of this contract depends crucially on the degree to which senior managers, from the CEO down, comply with it. They must act out the behaviors that they would like to see spread throughout the merging company. In terms of organizational behavior theory, this is a familiar idea: It is obviously important for leaders to 'walk the talk'.

In a merger context, however, there are some complicating factors. One such is the sudden presence of a large number of managers and employees who do not know you. Sky Chefs CEO Michael Kay seized the opportunity this presented. The company's pre-merger turnaround had been based on a performance contract involving an unusual combination of pervasive collaboration, intensive people development and tough performance management – not too far in some ways from the contract that Jack Welch had developed for General Electric. The challenge that Kay recognized, however, was the extension of this performance contract to the newcomers from Caterair. 'Sky Chefs brought into the process the cornerstones of its own behavior', Kay recalled. 'We said, "For this integration work to be successful we'll need to role model the behaviors we want to see in the new company and filter those messages back to the much larger audience that is sitting in the stands watching what's going on."'

Caterair's managers had a poor track record, but Kay reckoned that they could perform far better provided that the extremely stretching goals of the integration process were matched with detailed planning, practical tools and strong coaching support: 'And so we resourced the hell out of it and then said, "Look, here's what we expect you to accomplish. Here's the methodology we expect you to master. Here's the help we're going to give you to do that. There's no getting off the hook."'

Thus the success of Sky Chefs' acquisition was dependent on the ability of Caterair managers to stretch themselves as they had never done before. That in turn depended on the ability of Kay and his colleagues on the Sky Chefs side to model not just the performance standards *but also the willingness to stretch themselves*. A leader cannot realistically or fairly demand painful learning from others without visibly undergoing some of it himself. Kay himself saw this clearly:

> You know it's not so much about a test of leadership ability as it is about recognizing that you have a whole new audience that you are trying to influence. So the leadership behaviors you practice on your own field need to be held up to the light. Ask yourself: 'If I keep doing the things I've always done, how's it going to play over there where they don't know anything about me or my company or my value system or my culture?' If you're unwilling to even ask those questions of yourself then the likelihood of your changing anybody else is zero.

Kay's message is that the merger is an occasion for the demonstration by leaders of the cultural traits that really matter. Modeling change is a precondition for achieving it. As Steve Jones, MD of Suncorp-Metway, noted: 'You can't just stand up there and tell people what the new culture is going to be. You have to define in your mind what you want the new culture to stand for, do it for a little while, and then talk about what you have done. After that, any discussion on culture is a lot more credible.'

This is as much 'talking the walk' as 'walking the talk'. The flip charts that you and your colleagues fill with evocative phrases about the new culture are just the beginning: You will find that the stories you tell about enacting that culture connect far more powerfully with your people.

The new performance contract thus provides a valuable opportunity for the top team. As we saw in Chapter 2, it should have established itself as the 'template' of the new company before the close. The performance contract is a means of making that template concrete so that it can be applied across the management ranks.

The performance contract is critical for the retention of talented managers and employees no matter what specific retention steps are taken. Talent retention approaches vary by industry, by the type of talent, by the stage of the economic cycle, and by several other factors. In our interviews we found no strong consensus on what specific elements consistently work, but many CEOs were keen to tell us what does *not* work. The comments of Don Argus of BHP Billiton capture the general view: 'Buying loyalty with golden handshakes and similar devices does not work. People stay because they like the place and because they have a career. If they don't like it, they will leave anyway as soon as the options vest.' The simple, sobering truth is that in the long run, the appeal of the new company you are building will trump all other factors in determining the loyalty of talented employees. Temporary retention incentives are no substitute for a compelling performance contract.

In many mergers, talent retention demands intensive methodical work right from the beginning. You cannot achieve performance without a matching performance culture, and that requires a performance contract, which in return requires that you retain parties to the contract. Everything ultimately depends on having the people you need to make the new company work.

That is why Steve Kaufman recommends shifting the focus away from the tracking of retention rates – something that is often well done by companies that lose a lot of talent – to 'the identification of the top players in the period between the handshake and the signing. On announcement day you've got to be prepared to reach out to individuals you've already identified as critical.'

Approaches for sheltering the managers of an acquisition from the potentially stifling embrace of its new parent have become routine. Yet in protecting the acquired culture from change that is harmful you might inadvertently protect the acquirer from change within itself that is urgently needed. In some cases ensuring that the acquisition has a bracing effect on the acquirer's culture actually maximizes value. As we have seen, Swiss Bank Corp used its 1992 acquisition of the much smaller and more entrepreneurial O'Connor & Associates to catalyze change in itself. UBS Chairman Marcel Ospel described the dramatic impact in a speech in 2002:

We put young O'Connor managers in very senior SBC positions. The cultural reverse takeover was very courageous and painful. But its impact was phenomenal. It led to a sophistication and centralization of core management processes. It rejuvenated whole areas of the bank, and it set a new level of ambition and professionalism. The successful 'O'Connorization' inspired change in other areas of the bank.

UBS CEO Peter Wuffli told us that the humility that made this possible is 'probably the most distinctive element of our culture'. Beginning with the O'Connor acquisition 'we started to develop the openness to embrace change, to learn, and to not be too proud to adapt things'. In this case, the acquisition led to a revision in the performance contract across the global bank. Role modeling commitment to this revised contract was a central contribution of the bank's leaders.

Designing the Integration around the Performance Contract

The integration project should be managed in a way that mirrors the terms of the performance contract. Employees will naturally look upon the integration project's standards and processes for additional evidence of the kind of company you are creating. Lack of alignment between how the new company is supposed to work and how the integration project actually works could lead to a serious signaling problem. Don Argus gave an example: If you want to decentralize power in the new company, resist the temptation to concentrate it during the integration, even if that appears to be the most efficient way to run the project.

> **Managers and employees should be able to see the new performance contract operating in the internal workings of the integration project.**

There are many other subtle ways in which an integration project may send the wrong messages and thus interfere with the establishment of the performance contract. For example, the project may deflect the attention of managers and employees from the base business. Former Woolwich Bank CEO Lynne Peacock called this 'voyeurism'. As she led the integration after Barclays Bank bought the Woolwich in 2000, she found that the excitement of the integration process threatened to distract them from regular duties, particularly in serving customers:

These deals bring with them a degree of voyeurism that you have to stamp out. They're really exciting so everybody really wants to pitch in and that is actually where you get a performance dip. People want to be involved, but what they need to understand is that the way they can give us most value is just to get on and do their jobs.

Her message, in a nutshell, is to beware of generating an 'integration culture' rather than a performance culture.

Be wary, too, of fostering a 'culture culture', that is, a culture whose most prominent characteristic is a preoccupation with its own cultural traits. If what most animates managers and employees is the melding of their two cultures rather than how they can best collaborate to serve customers, then the merger will suffer. In fact, integrations may fail not just when the cultures clash, but also when both sides devote so much time to preventing their cultures from clashing that they lose their external orientation.

An integration is an inopportune time to undertake the risks of deep cultural introspection. Maintaining an external orientation is in any case a challenge during an integration because there are so many distractions. A deep exploration of corporate culture poses the same kind of risks no matter when it is undertaken. Therefore using the integration period as an opportunity to open up the corporate culture as a topic for intensive and lengthy debate simply doubles up the risk. It amounts to programmatic introspection at a particularly inopportune time.

On the other hand, momentum from a successful culture change effort undertaken before the merger can significantly increase the odds of succeeding with a highly ambitious integration plan, as we saw in the case of Sky Chefs in this chapter. Sir Richard Evans credited the British Aerospace Benchmark culture change program with this effect: 'Because of what we had achieved with the change program', he told us, 'a lot of the organization would have followed us through any scenario – anything we asked of them – in order to deliver what we wanted.'

Options for Cultural Intervention

The constant here is the need to establish a performance culture that is tightly linked to how value is to be created in the new company. The best way to achieve that goal may vary depending on the ways in which your company might respond to more or less overt cultural interventions. Just as the practice of medicine requires that the patient's general condition be taken into account before any treatment is undertaken, so you must assess the possibility of organizational side effects. As we have seen in this chapter, scoping the short-term cultural change aspirations too widely can backfire.

> **In general, intervention efforts focused on the performance culture have the best chance for success.**

Indeed, you might determine that it is best to avoid explicit discussion of culture altogether if it seems likely that this will be counterproductive in your company. CEO Dr. Daniel Vasella is widely credited for the cultural transformation of Novartis, both during the 1996 integration and in the years that followed. Yet he told us that he directed managers not to discuss culture and focus instead on performance. In his view it is possible to send cultural signals without talking directly about culture.

Only once did John McGrath talk explicitly about what the culture of Diageo should be. From the value statements of Grand Metropolitan and Guinness he distilled four values and then put his executives to work on refining them: 'I said "We're staying all through the night and all tomorrow until we fix this. Here are my values with descriptors for each. You can add descriptors if you want, but you have to use these four values." After a couple of hours and a bit of heat, we were done.'

A more elaborate approach was ultimately taken at HVB Group. Hans-Gert Penzel and his colleagues, as noted above, did not immediately notice the scale of cultural differences between the two merging Bavarian banks, but once these became clear they avoided an overreaction. As Penzel explained, they realized that it would take seven to ten years for two such cultures to converge fully, and that this is an emergent process that has its own natural pace. 'So when we found all this out after about six months we decided to identify the major cultural differences that were important to us, and wound up focusing on two or three values. We then promoted these with a systematic, top-down change management approach.'

As we have seen, at Amgen Kevin Sharer was also more interventionist, but in this case the acquisition was a fraction of the acquirer's size and the desired performance culture of the merged company did not materially differ from the culture that Amgen already had. Therefore Sharer's focus was on raising his own and his colleague's sensitivity to the Immunex corporate culture in order to retain the key talent needed to achieve a healthy merger.

These more interventionist approaches can pay off provided that they are focused on the performance culture needed for the new company and otherwise follow established principles for managing change.[4] Thus the best way to tackle culture – the locus of the most complex and intangible people issues – is to couple it tightly to the value creation objectives that led you to take on the merger in the first place.

CHAPTER 5

Championing External Stakeholders

Steve Boehm of Wachovia described to us the 'big-bang' model that had been followed for years in the US retail banking industry. All the changes to processes and systems would be introduced in a single weekend. If everything went well, on Monday morning customers from both sides would seamlessly adapt to the merged bank and very few would be lost to competitors. In practice, however, it is very difficult to pull this off for a merger of any size, and customers may find the transition very disruptive because they would need to become part of the elaborate big bang choreography with their new product features, new checkbooks, new ATM cards, new PINs, and the rest.

The big-bang model was designed to minimize complexity and cost for the merging banks, not to protect the customer experience. 'I think in the past', Boehm noted, 'a lot of banks would do mergers in a way that was very convenient for them, but not for the customer.'

When they started to take customers seriously the banks realized that operational economies were offset with at least temporary declines in customer satisfaction scores and, often, major defections. Wachovia's managers, however, expect an *increase* in customer satisfaction in a contemporary merger, which makes a lot of sense where the goal of the merger is to grow *beyond* the pro forma combined level of business for the two sides.

Boehm argues that an improvement in customer satisfaction becomes possible if the business changes experienced by the customer are separated from the systems conversion event. Changes to the two sets of products can be made early on so that the customers on both sides experience the merged bank's products and services before the system conversion takes place:

> We take care of new checks and so on ahead of the conversion window at a pace that is comfortable for customers. So they have time to come to understand the new product set and become familiar with it. The system change during the conversion weekend then becomes a perfunctory event that happens in the background. Customers are not even aware it is taking place.

The shift here is from a relatively unmanaged customer impact to a more managed one. Behind this shift lies the recognition that the merger puts customers in play along with other external stakeholders.

Lars Vig Larsen, the integration manager for the 2004 merger of Denmark's Group 4 Falck and the UK's Securicor to form security services giant Group 4 Securicor, told us that 'customers read newspapers like everybody else, but not very carefully. When we announce that we intend to merge, half of them think we have already done so. So any anxieties they may develop are already a serious problem on the day of announcement.'

One of the least predictable things in integration management is when and how customers and other external stakeholders will react to the merger. Much integration practice is based on the silent assumption that these stakeholders will remain out of the loop until contacted, and will then respond as predicted in the integration plan. This accounts for the widespread tactic of sheltering stakeholders as much as possible from the effects of the merger. The near-inevitability of some impact, and the positive opportunities for the company that this impact may actually provide, have been largely overlooked.

In the last two chapters, we focused on investors, financial analysts, managers and employees. These are the stakeholder groups that generally receive the most attention during an integration. This is quite understandable. Investors and financial analysts have a natural interest in how the merger will affect the prospects of one or both companies, and their concerns must be addressed systematically at the point of announcement. Managers and employees are of course charged with achieving the integration and may be strongly affected by it. These stakeholders are obviously important players in the integration drama.

Other stakeholders, such as customers, business partners, communities, labor unions and regulators, tend to be relatively neglected. This derives, in part, from the view that they should be sheltered as much as possible from the effects of the integration. 'Our merger is not their problem' is what we often hear.

The harsh reality is that sheltering often does not work well. Despite it, the merger event catches the attention of external stakeholders. One major manifestation of this is a decline of organizational focus on customers due to employees' preoccupation with the integration. Another is that competitors may woo your customers in the belief that you will be too distracted to hang onto them. That, in fact, may be an explicit part of their pitch: 'You might as well buy from us because these guys will be too bogged down with their merger to provide good service to you.'

It is wishful thinking to assume that customers and other stakeholders can be fully sheltered from the effects of your merger. In the real world, customers and other stakeholders become very alert to a major merger and very attuned to any fall-off in meeting their expectations. Competitors regularly exploit the distractions that mergers bring with them. Meanwhile those on the integration team charged with monitoring and protecting relationships with key stakeholders – if indeed such positions exist – are quickly overwhelmed by the challenge.

> **In many cases, attempting to shelter customers and other stakeholders from the effects of the merger will not work.**

In this frenzied climate opportunities not only to protect but also to strengthen key relationships with external stakeholders are usually overlooked. Indeed, it may even be possible to use those relationships to make the merger in particular and the company in general healthier.

Unfortunately, such opportunities are seldom seized, even by companies that otherwise excel at integration. Moreover, 'protecting' often turns out to mean neglecting, and this neglect eventually has deleterious effects on the base business. That is why it is not uncommon for companies to reassess downward the results of an apparently successful integration as it finally becomes apparent how damaging the loss of focus on the base business has been.

In Chapter 3 we noted that merger communications have become more sophisticated in recent years. Although we used the corporate story concept to highlight common weaknesses in communications, many companies now methodically communicate with at least some of the external stakeholder groups that are the subject of this chapter. However, communications with these groups is often rather mechanical and unimaginative. Moreover, very few companies see the opportunity to go beyond communications alone and energize or even transform key external relationships. Even managers who relish and excel at the dynamic challenge of interacting with customers and business partners may be surprisingly uncreative at engaging with the new external stakeholders that the merger brings on board. When we discuss detailed integration plans with managers, we often find that much less thought has been given to these external stakeholders.

The view that all these stakeholders can and should be sheltered from the merger has kept development here well-behind that of other integration challenges. Practice is relatively underdeveloped for external stakeholders because the deceptively straightforward expedient of sheltering has had such appeal for managers. The implicit view that integration is fundamentally about the internal organizational wiring of a company continues to impede progress, making external relationships a common trouble spot even in generally successful integrations.

We have seen that humility *vis-à-vis* one's merger partner is key to making any progress with cultural issues, and this is equally true for dealing with external stakeholders, but the point is perhaps not as obvious here. In the nature of things, the managers of two merging companies are always ill-prepared to deal with the arrival of new external stakeholders from the other side of the merger boundary. Recognizing that you know very little about these stakeholders is crucial, for what you do not know can indeed hurt you.

The humility that comes from that sobering recognition is ultimately liberating. It redirects your attention to a crucial value-creating activity: Identifying the small things in these relationships that you simply must get right in order to achieve a healthy merger.

Your leadership role here is complex and nuanced. You must encourage your managers to learn quickly and deeply about their new stakeholders at a hectic time when such learning is exceptionally difficult. You must also continuously redirect the two organizations' attention back to these stakeholders despite the distractions of the integration. For both groups, making the intellectual case is the easy part. Instilling energy and focus is much more demanding. Moreover, championing these stakeholders may require you to make some painful compromises around short-term integration goals – compromises for which you, as the leader, must take full responsibility.

What You Do Not Know Can Hurt You

Most of the time, the new sets of stakeholders that come with a merger seem pretty familiar: New customers who look like your current ones, new employees who look like your current ones, and so on. Our language often betrays our complacency here, as when we loosely extend the proper reach of the verb 'acquire' beyond the legally-owned assets of the other company to its customers and other stakeholder groups. As Eric Benhamou of 3Com cautioned: ' "Acquiring customers" is a very arrogant phrase. The customer has to *want* to be "acquired".'

Of course, no stakeholder can be simply 'acquired'. 'Wanting to be acquired' means committing to you by buying your products, investing in your shares, working for you, distributing your products, collaborating with you on research and development, and so on. Clearly it is dangerous to take such a commitment for granted by assuming that stakeholders will respond the way 'our' stakeholders normally do. When these differences are overlooked, important stakeholder groups beyond the corporate boundary in effect become orphans of the integration.

Organizational Health vs. Corporate Health

This neglect of external stakeholders reflects a tacit switch of objective from 'corporate health' to 'organizational health' – a *much* narrower concept involving only managers and employees. Whether a merger contributes to the overall health of your company depends upon a network of external stakeholders, not just upon the people that you employ.

This is not merely a fussy distinction: It can make a major practical difference. Narrowing the scope of 'health' can have adverse consequences because it may lead you to believe that a merger is not just healthy, but glowing with health, when actually a leadership intervention is urgently required. One bank's managers were targeting organizational health when they involved fully 30 per cent of their staff in an integration process. They saw this as an opportunity to catalyze change throughout the company, and the early signs indicated that they had indeed sparked a surge of positive energy. However, the staff and their managers were so excited by how things would be different in the new bank that they failed to attend sufficiently to customers, who in their turn noticed and began to take their business elsewhere. The grand irony here is that one of the important themes of the organization change initiative was the need for a stronger external orientation.

Talking about serving customers better is not the same as actually serving them better, and sometimes too much talk can be counterproductive. One of the important reasons that Compaq's 1998 acquisition of DEC failed, it is widely believed, is that the company used the integration as a forum for strategizing intensively about its aspirations for winning customers from IBM in the server market. Initially, the debates about how to do so were highly energizing, but over time the large, unwieldy integration office became mired in these debates. Meanwhile, Dell lured away customers in the low-end PC market and Compaq never recovered.

> **You cannot fully assess the health of a merger from inside the bounds of the integration project – or even from inside the bounds of the merging company.**

Diagnosing the health of a merger is not always a simple matter: appearance and reality may differ starkly. An integration that is buzzing with energy and conversations about customers could still be unhealthy. Its health cannot be determined solely on the basis of internal sources of information, you need to have a concrete sense of what is taking place out there, beyond the corporate boundary.

The Need for Crash Learning

Assessing the health of a merger requires rapid learning about the new customers and other external stakeholders that the merger brings in. Here we must confront the limits of experience. Yes, integration experience will help managers to get up to speed on these issues. Yet every major integration has its own distinctive challenges that require a fresh round of learning. For example, you may have integrated a dozen sales forces in the past, yet you still might not be able to identify immediately the pivotal, tacit features of the customer relationships of a new merger partner's sales force. You never know exactly what you have just bought – certainly not like you know your own company – and must undertake the integration without such exact knowledge.

3Com's Eric Benhamou noted, for example, that when he was new to mergers he found that many of his acquired companies tended to pay too much to their resellers given their limited role in the distribution chain. So he would move quickly to reduce or eliminate these payments. With experience he took a more measured approach:

> Whenever I tried to move too quickly there, I found it upsets the worlds of too many people and destroys personal relationships and trust. It alienates partners who may not have been pulling their weight all of the time but were still helpful. So I learned over time, that it's actually best to cut these people some slack and not capitalize on the cost savings opportunity right away. You have to allow the acquired company to get its footing, and then act later once you have everything in place and stable.

Thus hasty action could damage key relationships in unforeseeable ways.

In the fullness of time Benhamou's 'small things that you didn't know were there' make their appearance. Some of these are very small indeed. Benhamou offered another sales force example: 'The salesperson that you just moved to different accounts might just happen to have a great relationship with the secretary of a purchasing agent. That relationship might be essential for expediting a purchase order in an emergency. And that small thing, which is nowhere in the due diligence work that you do, has been lost because of that salesperson's transfer.'

Achievement of a healthy merger may require deep humility about what you know in multiple areas. You may not be able to predict where your competitors will conduct raids, and how. You might not know exactly what it is about your own or your partner's brand that is most in need of protection during the integration. You might not know where the opportunities lie to use the merger event to make relationships with customers and others stronger than ever (rather than just to protect them).

Every integration begins with a potentially dangerous lack of knowledge about the reaches that lie beyond the corporate boundary of the merging companies. Even if both companies know their own stakeholders extremely well, it will take time before this knowledge can be shared effectively across the combined management team. That is an aspect of integration – the development of a deeply-shared understanding of the merged company's external world – that receives too little attention in most integration plans.

> **Limited knowledge about external stakeholders poses serious risks that receive too little attention in many integration projects.**

Moreover, miscommunication can impede the sharing process. Your partner, for example, might not be able to describe the qualities of its brand with the precision that you require. Jean-François Pontal, who was named CEO of Orange and of the units of France Telecom with which it was merging in 2000, found that Orange's managers were actually rather poor at articulating the powerful brand's features:

> One thing that worked well in the end but was difficult was describing the Orange brand. People in Orange were not really able, for example, to distinguish between what applied generally to Orange and what was specific to the UK. They moved back and forth between these levels. So it became a process of elimination: 'This is Orange, that's not Orange.' It was all very difficult, but it did oblige the Orange people to understand themselves and their culture better.

Similarly, your partner may have functions and processes in place whose value is not immediately obvious to you. One transport company worked diligently to retain the customers of its acquired unit, but did not initially realize that a key account management system was crucial for this. Many key account managers left, together with their customers, before the important role that this system had played was recognized.

IT of course is an area where it is easy to antagonize customers inadvertently – with or without a merger. Just small changes in format and procedures can drive away customers who perceive them as an imposition. Pricing strategy is another potential alienator: Even small adjustments to harmonize the two companies' pricing systems can cause outsize anger and defections. The same holds for territory allocations. The small things that can cause so much havoc take many forms and differ from one integration to the next.[1]

Learning how the corporate system works beyond the corporate boundary is thus a key challenge for achieving a healthy merger. It requires tenacity, because a merging company tends to turn inward and make integration decisions without consideration for external stakeholders. In such a setting it can be very difficult even to identify the small things at risk, not to speak of fixing them.

Listening to External Stakeholders

Ultimately, learning in this difficult context requires an energetic effort to listen and a sufficiently open mind to challenge any initial assumptions you may have about what drives these stakeholders. You may be surprised to find that their interests and concerns are very different from what you had supposed them to be.

> **External stakeholders will almost always provide striking information with direct relevance to the health of your merger if you take the trouble to listen to them.**

For example, during the integration of Sky Chefs with Caterair, Michael Kay found that many of Caterair's customers had no worries about the new company and readily signed the consents needed to transfer their contracts to Sky Chefs. But some did worry. 'So we spent more time with them', Kay told us, 'We talked a lot about the integration strategy, and told them that Caterair people were going to be treated no differently than Sky Chefs' people. Sometimes we even got into the details of how we were going to put jobs up for bid.'

It might seem strange that a corporate customer would care about the fairness of the job appointments process in one of its suppliers. Yet that is precisely the kind of small thing that is so difficult to anticipate. Moreover, often when such a small thing crops up, it demands a spontaneous, effective response.

When Norsk Hydro bought VAW Aluminum from Germany's E.On AG in 2002, the acquisition's managers told their new parent that the labor unions had no interest in corporate strategy. All they cared about was the number of jobs that would be cut in Germany. Eventually top managers met with forty union representatives and invited them to ask whatever was on their mind. Tore Torvund, an Executive Vice President at Norsk Hydro, recalled the surprising range of issues that the unions raised:

> We could have continued the whole night. They asked questions about the strategy for the next five years. Will there be more acquisitions? What about the corporate structure? Where will the headquarters be in the future? Why did we relocate some office functions, and was that really cost-efficient? And so on. And I said to myself: We should have done this two months ago.

Sometimes stakeholders' concerns can be magnified by local conditions that the acquirer may know nothing about. John McGrath recalled how a member of the Scottish parliament took the floor to praise Diageo's sensitive handling of the closure of their Dumbarton factory. Yet this followed a much smaller closure in Perth that had triggered a brief but feisty public backlash against the company. Much of the difference in reactions can be accounted for in terms of improvements in Diageo's processes, but McGrath noted that another company in an unrelated industry had just laid off employees in Perth as a result of another merger. For Diageo, this was an unconnected event, but evidently not for the local community.

Better management of risks is not the only benefit from listening. External stakeholders may help your company in a variety of surprising ways. For example, they may have useful suggestions for your company's future. Eric Benhamou told us some of his acquisition ideas originated from his customers:

> They would say 'In order to solve my networking problem I had to use some of your products as well as products from this other company. Why don't you buy them? That way I could buy the entire network from you and you could give me a single service contract for the whole thing. It would simplify the way I do business with you. And then I could also deploy it in Asia and Eastern Europe knowing that you'd stand behind it.'

The risks of growth through acquisition obviously decline when your customers are eager to see you do the deal. In fact, they will interpret it as a commitment to them.

Of course it is helpful to have a deep understanding of your customers' and business partners' interests and concerns, and the business you do directly with them will certainly provide plenty of clues. Nevertheless, the stakes for these stakeholders may be of a very different kind than you might imagine.

Every stakeholder has a circle of interests and concerns that extends well-beyond the practical confines of your current working relationship with them. Any competent salesperson knows that getting to know the customer involves developing a sense of this broader identity. Unfortunately, during a merger there is a strong temptation to stick to what you need them to know and to de-emphasize listening and learning that could be important for the success of the integration and beyond.

Resist the temptation.

Getting the 'Small Things' Right

Perhaps the simplest yet most effective way to give yourself a chance to get these small things right is to avoid overburdening the integration in ways that can lead to customer problems. The small things require attention, a resource that is at a stiff premium during an integration.

> **Getting the 'small things' right during an integration requires significant attention at a time when it is hard to spare.**

John McGrath of Diageo recalled that reorganizing brand management during the integration caused a loss of momentum. The challenge of spreading brand expertise across the merger boundary was more than enough to keep the brand managers busy for months. But McGrath and this team demanded more: 'We should have left the brand people to get on with it and we shouldn't have messed around with them. We should have said, "You're running the brands, you carry on. Your job is to teach half the company by definition. In each country you go to, half the people won't know about the brand, roughly speaking, and half will. So just do that." ' In a largely successful integration, McGrath cited this as the single significant area where with hindsight he would have acted differently. In the context of a complex, worldwide integration process, the role of brand managers in spreading brand expertise was surely a small thing, but in the end it mattered.

Similarly, Peter Wuffli of UBS noted that in the 1998 merger with Swiss Bank Corp they integrated quickly across the board but should have moved more slowly for private banking and asset management. In those areas 'the hurried speed of integration probably created more damage than the value it produced.'

Getting the small things right also requires rigorous analysis of them. After Ford's 1999 acquisition of Volvo, managers diligently defined the multiple small things that together made the Volvo brand so powerful. They comprehensively analysed what protection of the brand would concretely mean in terms of processes, standards, pricing and so on. What does the Volvo's status as a premium brand mean for pricing relative to other group products? What does Volvo's commitment to world-class safety standards mean for the way the safety function is structured and run? Because answers to these and other pertinent questions were definitively documented, not only was the brand fully protected but also the integration team was able to focus its search for synergies more efficiently. The managers had carefully roped off areas that needed to remain off limits.

In general, keeping brands distinct requires attention to small things. The co-existence in the merged company of two brands generally poses the risk of weakening either or both as the differences between them become blurred. There is far more involved in keeping them distinct than the way the product or service is positioned in advertising.

For example, one tough challenge is determining how far down the organization to integrate the management of two brands. When Barclays Bank bought the Woolwich Bank in 2000, it resolved to maintain the strength of both brands while integrating where appropriate. As Lynne Peacock explains, when two brands are under a single corporate roof it may not be obvious how far integration should go:

> At what level should things be put together and at what level should they remain separate? You've really got to take a view on that. Because in truth I think it's perfectly possible for a person to head up all retail banking after the acquisition. And it is also possible for someone to head up all branch distribution. But at what point must you keep it separate if you're going to make sure the thing runs properly? Can you honestly expect a branch manager whom you pay £20,000 a year to have the skills to manage two different kinds of customer experience within a single branch?

Thus the decision to maintain two brands in the merged company may raise a series of difficult questions around where and how to integrate associated people, systems and processes. A merger, in fact, may bring to light the degree to which the vitality of brands depends upon a host of small things.

Protecting the operational and organizational factors that make a brand successful can make a decisive difference in the health of a merger.

It is therefore not surprising that these and other small things sometimes demand a disproportionate amount of senior management decision-making time during an integration.

Tough Calls on the Small Things

So far we have emphasized caution about the small things. It may seem tempting to opt for a 'maximalist' approach to brand protection that slows the integration down significantly wherever the brand is at risk.

In some cases, however, this may be the approach that actually provides the *least* protection to the brand. Hans-Gert Penzel, who led the 1998 integration that created Germany's Bayerische Hypotheken und Vereinsbank (now HVB Group), noted that while his retail customers were largely unconcerned by the merger, his wholesale customers expected rapid consolidation of the dealing rooms and wanted immediate clarity about their credit lines and their points of contact in the bank. Their worries began on the day of the announcement when they read about the deal in the financial press, and remained acute until their post-integration arrangements were fully clarified.

> **Some of the toughest calls are around the 'small things'.**

Some of the tough calls you make to get the small things right might not appear to be correct to colleagues – even in retrospect. After Barclays' acquisition of Woolwich, eighteen months passed before integration began in earnest. We asked Lynne Peacock whether a much faster integration would have been better. As so often, it is hard to close the debate definitively, because one can only speculate on the road not traveled. She argued that the small things that matter to customers could be at risk during a rapid integration:

> Barclays people did not necessarily completely understand everything that existed at the Woolwich. I don't mean some wonderful pearls of wisdom but rather the fundamental difference in the customer experience, in the things that touch the customer. I don't think that difference would have been appreciated and it just needed time. It's a bit like saying Fords and Jaguars are cars and therefore why are we messing around? You really need to understand who's buying a Ford and who's buying a Jaguar – and why.

In our experience, the senior managers who have exerted the most effort to understand their own customers are the most circumspect about their knowledge of what makes their partner's customers tick. Even where there is a strong overlap in the two companies' customers, they do not assume that the customers buy from both companies for the same reasons. They are free agents – free to play on someone else's team – and if the merger leads to a reduction in the quality of service or even to a neutral but irritating change in the way the service is delivered, they may well go elsewhere.

There is nothing quite like a poorly executed merger integration to reveal the limited sense in which customers are 'ours'. And we have noticed over the years the paradox that companies with the strongest 'ownership' of their customers are precisely those that are most humble about that ownership. As a general rule, these companies prefer to err on the side of caution in managing those parts of the integration that deal with customers.

Getting the small things right is most obviously important where revenue gains are targeted. After all, in these cases the success of the merger depends upon the customer deciding to act differently. Managers of course recognize how important it is to influence customers' buying decisions.

However, these considerations apply to *all* mergers, including those that are not targeting revenue gains. Revenue protection is always an issue to some degree because there are so many small things that could impinge on the customer experience. If you are not continuously asking the integration team about the impacts of the proposed steps on that experience, why should the team consider those impacts important?

Not Just Customers

These considerations apply with no less force to business partners such as suppliers, distributors and joint venture partners. Mergers often have a significant impact on these partners as, for example, sources of supply are consolidated and product lines are integrated.

Yet many senior managers pay little heed to this. They seem content with simply announcing the (often negative) consequences of the integration to their business partners – which of course means not treating them like partners at all.

> **Many external stakeholder groups require attention during an integration – not just customers.**

Although the same care in handling customers may be needed for business partners, the two groups may respond to the merger in very different ways.

For example, a manufacturer decided to keep both brands after acquiring a competitor with a similar product line. It was correct in its assessment that both brands were viable in terms of customer demand. What it failed to take into account is that some of its distributors were nevertheless reluctant to carry both lines because they believed that customers saw the brands as largely interchangeable. So this company's revenue protection steps were less effective than planned. As with any other stakeholder group, your business partners must be understood on their own terms.

Relationships with business partners may also be vulnerable to some inadvertent impacts of the integration. One consumer goods company was concerned about retaining its managers during a regulatory investigation of its merger. It therefore decided to double their bonus. As a consequence, those managers overstocked product with retailers during the bonus period – a serious irritant at exactly the wrong time. So getting the small things right requires anticipation of the external impact of such internal changes as a revision of the bonus system.

The Leadership Challenge

It is a sad irony that even companies whose external orientation has brought them the financial success needed to fund an M&A program often allow that orientation to erode during integrations. They already do systematically much that we recommend in this chapter – *except during an integration.* Integrations often feel like an intramural event with very high walls. There is nothing quite like a merger to induce a company to look inward.

Although one class of external stakeholders – investors and financial analysts – have benefited from sharply increased attention in recent years, for other stakeholder groups the record is uneven. To be sure, companies in industries that are strongly customer-focused seem to have made more progress in managing customer relationships. Broadly speaking, however, there remains a tendency during an integration for the map of corporate concerns to contract to match the formal boundaries of the merging company. The land of customers, business partners, communities, labor unions and regulators almost becomes *terra incognita.*

Moreover, it is difficult to make progress in keeping external stakeholders on board because their salient characteristics – their externality, diversity, and fluidity – make it hard to diagnose the specific challenges posed by an integration. Integrators that master the challenges of one group (such as retail customers) might still struggle with another (such as suppliers). This is therefore an area where managers may easily be blindsided.

We believe that the active championing of external stakeholders is key. 'Active championing' requires much more than perfunctory mention of the importance of these stakeholders in standard forums such as the integration kick-off meeting. We cannot specify the precise steps that championing would consist of in any concrete case, because that, of course, depends on the specific 'small things' that make rapid learning so necessary during an integration. Nevertheless, we offer three recommendations that we have seen make a positive difference fairly regularly.

- **Do not flinch from taking on the problem of corporate arrogance.** Taking external stakeholders for granted during a merger may betray a belief that they are docile and predictable – rather than the active, astute pursuers of their own interest that they often prove to be. The punishing pace of an integration cannot by itself explain how diligent value-maximizing managers could treat key stakeholders like orphans for weeks or months. In all too many cases, at least temporarily these stakeholders are not accorded the respect they deserve.

  Such arrogance can take many subtle forms. There may be deep pride in a brilliantly conceived and negotiated deal that is blind to the role that external stakeholders must ultimately play in the success of any merger. Or it may be more exciting and personally gratifying to have investment bankers, major investors and financial analysts listen to you than it is to switch roles and listen yourself to customers and business partners. The latter may seem a bit like hometown friends who lack the glamorous aura of the wheeler-dealer crowd. Moreover, notable past success in winning over customers or business partners may lead you to believe that you have them fully under control – an attitude that can be as disastrous in business as it is in personal relationships.

  When cast in such bald terms, it is obvious to any manager that such arrogance is wrongheaded and dangerous. In normal times, it is challenging enough to avoid such an unhealthy attitude and the behaviors that go with it, but mergers are trying periods when the discipline of corporate humility tends to break down. That is why, for example, we so often see the 'A team' of senior managers busy discussing the new company's strategy with players in the newly-attentive financial markets while the 'B team' of PR people and other staffers are left to attend to the needs of customers and other orphans of the integration.

  Such patterns of behavior of course make no business sense. To combat them, you must expose the arrogance in which they are rooted.

  In general, your best course is forcefully and repeatedly to remind managers from both sides of the merger boundary of the business realities that make such arrogance foolhardy. For example, if your channel partners are aligned with your vision, as outsiders they will be more credible exponents of it in the marketplace than you as an insider could possibly be.

Tirelessly conveying this message may make you feel uncomfortably preachy, and at times you may indeed come across that way. Yet that is a small price to pay for managing the risks of corporate arrogance during a merger.

■ **Set out with the determination to improve stakeholder relationships and to strengthen the company's external orientation**. Warning about arrogance is not enough: It does not provide enough positive guidance for the new company. Nor does it energize the organization. Who can get excited about limiting the merger's damage to your customer base?

At Group 4 Securicor, CEO Lars Norby recognized that a stronger customer orientation was needed for the new company, particularly in their European operations. He and his top team therefore presented the merger as an opportunity to perform demonstrably better in this area than either predecessor company had done. As a result, in one of their biggest countries, the UK, they actually managed to lower the customer churn rate from pre-merger levels. This is a far cry from the usual goal of keeping the increase in the churn rate to a 'respectable' level.

To accomplish this, the company systematically applied all the standard customer-retention techniques (segmentation of customers, use of multiple communication channels, contact immediately after announcement, and so on). Norby acknowledged that these were essential. Yet what ultimately made the difference was the high aspiration level:

> We decided that this was a great opportunity to get closer to our customers. So from the beginning we were after much more than the usual goal of just not losing them. After all, the merged company is a new platform with a lot of uncertainties. This is a new world for us. The existing norms are under pressure, so we decided to use this time to establish some new ones.

This is a fairly unusual case where the merger actually led to a stronger external orientation. Norby saw that conspicuous success during the integration could be transformative: 'If we could show our people out there that not only have we succeeded in not losing customers, but that by being much more pro-active with them and really listening to them we have actually increased retention, then this would have a powerful demonstration effect for the future.'

Championing external stakeholders in this way makes strong business sense for three reasons. First, the more positive tone of the outreach effort will increase its effectiveness. Stakeholders would rather be enthused than merely pacified. Second, it establishes from the start the kind of external orientation that the new company will need to prevail in the marketplace. That way, there will not be any need to recover that orientation after the integration ordeal has weakened it. Third, the emphasis on external orientation gives the two sides something positive on which to collaborate, thereby helping to bring the new company together. As we saw in Chapter 2, this effect may emerge spontaneously in the presence of an external crisis, but it is of course preferable to lead them to it without a crisis.

■ **Enlist for the outreach effort strong managers who have relevant experience and contacts**. You cannot hope to champion these external stakeholders without expert help. Mergers between state health insurers in the United States require formal approval from the insurance commissioners in each state. In addition, there are many other stakeholders in the healthcare system – doctors, hospitals, communities, patients, employers, and local legislators – who may have a strong interest in the outcome. Therefore when the two large multi-state health insurers Anthem and Wellpoint agreed to merge in 2004, CFO Mike Smith of Anthem and his colleagues developed an elaborate strategy for reaching out to all of these stakeholder groups. Because of the ongoing and exceptionally complex challenge of managing external stakeholder relationships in this industry, large health insurers are generally well organized to discuss their mergers. They already have the right people with the right relationships in place, as Smith noted:

> We need to know, for example, what the American Medical Association will say about the deal. And so we put an esteemed, nationally recognized clinician on planes to go talk to the leadership of the AMA and of other medical societies. And then we put our regulatory staff – which includes former state commissioners and others with standing among the National Association of Insurance Commissioners – on the ground to go talk to state commissioners. We also put our account management and operating team on notice, with talking points to respond to the concerns that they may hear from our accounts or from others. So it's a very elaborate effort.

In this industry, the kinds of small things we have been discussing in this chapter receive regular attention. In most industries, however, preparing to engage with external stakeholders may require some painful adjustments. Eric Benhamou noted, for example, that merging sales forces with minimal damage to external relationships requires 'an extremely experienced, soft-touch sales executive who has been through many of these things before'. Such a person will of course be hard to spare from his or her regular role.

*   *   *

We suggest that you need to 'champion' these stakeholders because this is as much about role modeling as it is about acting. While we believe that direct engagement with external stakeholders is vital, in reality you are unlikely to be the one that discovers the many small things that are so pivotal to all these relationships.

That is why your role modeling is so important. Managers and employees who might be preoccupied with the internal stresses of the integration need to be reminded that health of the merger ultimately depends at least as much on people that are not being 'integrated' as on those who are. The people issues 'out there' among customers, business partners, communities, labor unions and regulators may affect the value created in the merger in subtle but powerful ways.

CHAPTER 6

Fostering Momentum and Learning

During Steve Kaufman's tenure as CEO from 1986 to 2000, Arrow Electronics developed its post-merger management capabilities to the point where it could complete an integration at breakneck speed. Kaufman and SVP Betty Jane Scheihing, his *de facto* head of integration, kept up the pace throughout each integration but were particularly active in the days immediately before and after the announcement.

Before signing, Kaufman and his counterpart CEO at the target would produce a video that introduced the deal. Two copies were shipped to each Arrow branch manager, timed to arrive just before the announcement. Each package would include instructions that it was not to be opened until the recipient received a call from Arrow headquarters (as the deal might fall through at the last minute). When the call arrived that confirmed that the deal has been signed (usually on a Saturday), the Arrow manager was instructed to deliver the second videotape to the target's local branch manager. Meanwhile, general managers would receive a 'pitch pack' to present to their branches, and the senior managers of Arrow and the target would meet to identify the target's top few dozen critical players.

Then Kaufman would announce the transaction – typically on a Monday – to the media, the financial community, and the workforces of the two companies. Several hours later, he would be at the target's headquarters, and from there he would move on to the dozen or so cities where it has major locations. In tandem with this, the president of Arrow North America would cover places not on Kaufman's itinerary, while the head of supplier relationships would visit key suppliers to pitch the deal.

On the day following the announcement, every Arrow and target employee would receive a letter at home that explained the transaction in general terms. Also, Kaufman would send his 'fire spotter' to the target's headquarters with the formal mandate of heading up IT integration and acting as a liaison with the target's management. This person also had the informal mandate of keeping his or her ears to the ground, of spotting problems early, and of developing enough of an insider's view of the company to be able to assess, for example, which managers are marginal, which do the heavy lifting, and which might be inclined to try to undermine the deal. At the same time, the 'Arrow War Room' – a small conference room that served as the merger process information center – would be opened for business. The names of critical players both of the target and of Arrow would be posted on a large magnetized control panel that served to track the overall status of detailed retention efforts.

All this would happen within a few days.

These efforts could move fast in part because so much spadework would have been done before the announcement. Although sales people and sales managers would not be allowed to talk to their counterparts at that time, regional sales executives would get together to discuss relative strengths and weaknesses in different market segments, in different geographic markets, and in relationships with specific suppliers. Because they would swap as much information as is legally permissible, Arrow often approached and sometimes actually met the goal of fully integrating on the day of closing.

Yet when Arrow acquired Anthem Electronics in 1994, it throttled back the speed so much that almost nothing at all happened in the first year. Says Kaufman: 'I kept it separate and went around making speeches saying "My name is Steve. Separate is good!"'

In an industry where the trend towards centralization was strong, Anthem had maintained a highly decentralized approach. Not only did buying take place in the field, but they also continued to maintain branch warehouses after other distributors had rationalized them. This older business model had higher costs, but also enabled Anthem to build deep relationships with some important customers that strongly preferred it. So Kaufman allowed Anthem to retain its decentralized model indefinitely. 'I was prepared to leave it separate until their management said, "We don't want to be separate any more."'

After about a year, the Anthem managers admitted that their inventory costs were much too high, so they centralized warehousing. Yet the two sets of inventory were not actually combined in Arrow's facility. Rather, Anthem's inventory was kept separate as a 'warehouse within a warehouse'.

After three years, Anthem's top manager reported that the arm's-length – or by now, forearm's-length – arrangement was not working any more. The sales teams were beginning to compete more with each other than with their external competitors, and internal competition had reached dangerous levels. He suggested combining the teams. Kaufman came up with another solution that involved segmenting the market by customer type, and this brought the problem under control.

Kaufman and his team have developed what many might consider to be best-practice capability at maximizing integration speed, but he put that capability in a larger context where it is a conscious choice, not an automatic routine:

> I am aware that the mantra about integration is to do it fast, because only speed will effectively recapture the value of the transaction. And we do it faster than anybody when necessary. Nevertheless our deals are always done for strategic reasons, not for incremental earnings per share. We are focused on the long view. If we have a year or two of dilution or a year or two of not capturing the synergies of a deal, we're prepared to live with that in order to make sure we have the base set.

Kaufman set the pace according to the ability of both Arrow and Anthem managers to learn how to accommodate the Anthem business model within Arrow. If he had simply defined the integration 'end-game' and immediately moved towards it, he might well have destroyed value even if his idea of the end-game were exactly right. He might have lost so much key Anthem talent and weakened the value proposition for Anthem's customers to such an extent that the merger would have been unhealthy as a whole despite the accelerated cost savings from rapid integration. The need for learning did indeed slow down the integration, but it did not, strictly speaking, hamper momentum. On the contrary: building the understanding and commitment among the acquisition's managers was a critical contributor to that momentum.

This of course is an outlier case where the need for learning dictated a significant deceleration in the integration. Learning may also require a narrowing of the *scope* of the integration (as we saw in the case of UBS's acquisition of O'Connor in Chapter 3, where many of the traits of the acquired unit were carefully preserved) or a softening of its *style* (as we saw in the case of 3Com in Chapter 5, where Eric Benhamou spoke of the need for a 'soft-touch' sales executive to manage the integration of the sales forces). Most of the time, however, learning will not require the radical deceleration of the integration timetable that makes the Anthem case so striking.

Sometimes, in fact, such learning must be achieved at breakneck speed. When British Aerospace and Marconi Electronic Systems merged in 1999, the operational overlaps between the two companies turned out to be so minimal that the £275 million in synergies that had been promised to the markets were simply unattainable. Yet the integration ultimately brought in £400 million in savings because the integration team redirected its attention to procurement and other areas where major savings were possible. This is 'unfreezing'– the use of the integration as a catalyst for exploiting valuable change opportunities that have been available all along but somehow were never addressed. Taking advantage of this opportunity turned a failing integration into a major success, as Mike Turner noted: 'With unfreezing you're using the opportunity of a merger to take best practice from outside and apply it – something that you could do at any time. Frankly, I reckon two-thirds of what we've achieved in financial terms is from unfreezing, not from synergy – just by doing things differently.'

Of course there was learning entailed in the identification of these savings opportunities. Yet there was also a deeper level of learning as the company's managers responded to the synergy shortfall. Integration manager Alistair Imrie described it to us in the following way:

> I think the recognition that we were going to have to do things
> fundamentally differently gave us a breakthrough. Once we stopped
> concerning ourselves about the fact that synergies would only produce
> a relatively limited amount of the savings, then all of a sudden we
> started to really get our minds around the fact that we were just going
> to have to behave differently, organize differently and all the rest of it.
> We convinced ourselves that we had the strength of purpose and the
> will to do it, and we built ourselves a significant degree of confidence
> in the way to overcome challenges to the process.

This discovery by the team of what it was capable of was pivotal for the integration's success because it secured momentum that the shortfall in synergies had imperiled.

It can be painful to recognize, as in the Arrow Electronics case, that one's most impressive capabilities are not always applicable. It can also be initially difficult to accept, as in the BAE Systems case, that one must be open to searching analysis of a range of business processes – the way things have always been done – that are not directly connected to the integration. What these two very different cases share is the fact that deeply self-reflective learning was required. In each case *corporate self-knowledge* made a pivotal contribution to the ultimate health of the merger.

On the face of it, an integration would appear to be a poor learning environment. There are too many tensions and uncertainties, and the pace is too relentless. Time is too short, the deadlines too demanding. Slowing down to learn appears to be a luxury – or even a serious risk.

Most managers consider learning, which basically consists of acquiring new knowledge or unlearning previous bad habits, as a lower priority than momentum. They believe that much learning can better be undertaken after the integration period, when the tempo has slowed again. The knowledge thus acquired retrospectively can be embedded in ongoing operations or, where it is specific to M&A, can be held in reserve for the next integration. *Just get it done. Hold off on learning until later. Then make sure you do it better the next time.*[1]

The consensus view is thus that there is a severe trade-off between momentum and learning, and that the emphasis should be squarely on momentum during the integration – particularly in the crucial early weeks or months. Such a view would limit learning to urgent and highly pragmatic knowledge-sharing in such areas as the product lines and customer bases of the two companies.

That view has some merit, but achievement of a healthy merger may well depend on your ability to recognize its limits. In most mergers there will be some challenging learning that you *must* undertake in order to protect the value creation objectives of the merger. In other words, momentum and learning are not inherently in conflict, and sometimes the only way to achieve both is to go after both.

> **Deferring learning for the sake of momentum is not always wise because some learning may be 'integration-critical'.**

Most often, as in the Arrow and BAE Systems cases, the key challenge is to develop and apply corporate self-knowledge.

Beyond Speed: Momentum and Learning

Not so long ago, there was much discussion among integrators of the simple question 'How fast should we integrate?' This has changed. In general, we find that although experienced managers today put great emphasis on integration speed they are well-aware that pacing an integration requires attention to momentum and learning as well. They also see this as one of the most complex challenges they face during a merger.[2]

The Perils of Speed

'Put me in the camp that says you should go as fast as possible', Don Argus of BHP Billiton told us. That camp has a lot of leaders in permanent residence.

Yet many of our interviewees pointed out that it is subject to many qualifications. Argus himself offered one qualification, noting that the phrase 'as fast as possible' may mean different things depending upon the type of merger. For example, cost-driven mergers can generally go faster than revenue-driven ones, but even the latter can sometimes go fast when the value is to be created in re-pricing. David Shedlarz of Pfizer added that there might be reasons for adopting a different pace for different parts of the organization or for different geographic areas. Kevin Sharer of Amgen told us that keeping to a disciplined schedule makes more sense than continually pushing for maximum speed, while Michael Kay of Sky Chefs, who inculcated a faster pace into his company's corporate culture in the early 1990s, cautioned that it is better to focus on planning thoroughly and on providing the right resources than on abstract arguments about speed. Dr. Daniel Vasella of Novartis offered another caution. He told us that the pacing of an integration ultimately requires intuition about what the company can bear, and we should recognize that change takes time. 'I cannot change myself in three months. How could I expect a company to change in that time?'

There are indeed many reasons for *not* driving the integration at full speed. One of the most important is the need to rapidly deepen your knowledge of your partner so that the integration can be conducted in a way that minimizes critical risks and identifies important opportunities.

> **The sound general prescription of integrating quickly is subject to numerous qualifications.**

One feature common to most reasons for proceeding deliberately is a knowledge gap of some kind. You do not know something about your partner, or they do not know something about you. Or you lack a shared understanding of your combined customer base and business relationships. Or you do not know how to combine product and service lines, or how to make tough choices between your personnel, systems, processes, locations and so on. Or external stakeholders, such as customers, regulators, communities and labor unions, do not understand what is changing for them.

Every integration requires a large number of changes that affect many actors to varying degrees, and coping with these changes requires substantial learning. The popular perception that integration is fundamentally an exercise in rigorous execution is flawed. Integration is a highly learning-intensive activity. People often do not think of it in this way because much of the required change involves learning that is pretty straightforward. It seems that simple communication of what is different is all that is needed. The merging company with all its stakeholders is thus imagined as a large machine, and the integration task as a giant exercise in reprogramming the machine.

Yet learning is not always so straightforward. In fact, as we have seen repeatedly in earlier chapters, learning is the major wild card of integration pacing. It is the intangible factor that most complicates the decision on how fast to go. Most of the disruptions to momentum involve the failure of some party to learn quickly and well.

In our view, too little attention is paid to such breakdowns in integration-critical learning. Admittedly, there is wisdom in the objective of simplifying the integration challenge by deferring ambitious learning initiatives wherever feasible until after the integration. Yet this of course applies only to learning that is *not* strictly critical to the achievement of integration goals.

The Scope and Limits of Post-Integration Learning

The importance of integration-critical learning, and the halting progress that has been made in defining and undertaking it, can be highlighted through contrast. *Post-integration learning* is an area where integrators have made particularly impressive progress in recent years. How do its challenges contrast with those of integration-critical learning, and why are integrators making relatively little progress with the latter?

The practice of retrospectively capturing and applying lessons learned from an integration is one of the strongest differentiators between merely competent integrators and those that get better with each merger round. In fact, in our survey an established routine for systematically examining both the integration process and its outcomes emerged as *the* single most important differentiating factor among the more than fifty factors that we analysed. By contrast, significant integration experience did not have the expected 'learning curve' effect: the level of such experience was an insignificant predictor of merger results. What really matters, it seems, is not so much how many mergers you have done before as how methodically you invest in learning from them.[3]

> **The case for investing heavily in systematic post-integration learning is unassailable.**

Among effective integrators we continue to see much interesting innovation around the formal disciplines that make this learning possible. At 3Com, for instance, Eric Benhamou reviewed the acquisition track record on an annual basis by going all the way back to the original management presentations that were used to justify the deals. This contrasts with the more common practice of comparing results only with formal targets established at the beginning of the integration. Benhamou's reality check against the initial value expectations for the transaction is more likely to yield up learning – especially about M&A strategy – than review of the integration process alone.

Part of the challenge of learning from past integrations in global companies is making the lessons learned accessible for all who need to consult them. To address this, David Shedlarz ensured that the integration templates from prior Pfizer mergers were posted online. This included, for example, detailed notes from leaders of the transitions teams. In this way managers could readily consult a rigorously structured compendium of experience for any new deal.

A related challenge is to ensure that this knowledge is granted the respect it deserves. At Shell, Greg Hill told us that managers who plan to depart from the codified lessons learned from prior acquisitions are required to provide a formal rationale to the executive committee.

The lessons from an integration may of course increase the possible speed of the next one, but there is still the problem that an integration approach that is deeply familiar to one side may be completely new to the other. To address this, Steve Boehm of Wachovia told us that the bank had hired a library science specialist to document the highly successful 2001 merger between First Union and Wachovia so that future integrations could get a strong start. As he noted, 'it is very important that the two partners understand one another quickly in terms of how they're going to approach the mountain of work that has to be done. We think that documenting our approach and making sure it remains a living document saves weeks if not months of learning on the front end of an integration.'

In addition to formally codified learning, mergers spawn a huge amount of tacit learning that must be retained for future use. As Steve Jones of Suncorp-Metway noted, 'the real experience is in people's heads, and it's impossible to write it all down. So we purposefully hung onto many of the people who were involved in our first merger because it was such a success. We used them again in the next one, and that made a big difference.'

Hans-Gert Penzel of HVB Group argued forcefully for both comprehensive codification and the continued access to the holders of tacit knowledge. His team documented their integration approach in a published book backed by thousands of pages of proprietary detail. Yet for any future merger he would still reach out for experienced integration hands: 'If we announced a big merger today I would be able to get together within a day fifty people who know how to do it.'

As important as these integration experts are, however, veterans of integrations consistently highlight the important role of line managers. In particular, line ownership is seen as the key variable that determines whether or not momentum can be sustained after the integration formally ends. Eric Benhamou of 3Com, for example, argued that the achievement of line ownership is so important that it constitutes a condition for doing a deal: 'You shouldn't do an acquisition simply because corporate wants to do it. There has to be a sponsoring organization that wants it badly enough that they're willing to be accountable for it.'

Many experienced acquirers, such as Cisco and Intel, have established a dual 'championing' structure for each acquisition: A 'process' champion responsible for the coordination of the planning and implementation phases, and a 'business' champion who owns the key business decisions and drives the operations and P&L of the acquired unit. This allows a balance between the process and line ownership of the merger from well before the announcement through to the formal transfer of complete control to the line manager.

In general, the sooner the line takes over responsibility for the integration's processes and goals, the better. One of the subtle yet powerful reasons for this is that it ensures that there is a set of managers who have experience of *both* the integration *and* the long-term results of the integration. They are in an especially strong position to recognize in retrospect what worked well and what did not.

Many companies could benefit greatly from applying the discipline of post-integration learning with more energy and creativity. Both the formal research and our experience confirm that this is a major differentiator in integration success.

These advances are possible because the post-integration environment is favorable for learning. When the integration is over, the pressures ease and it is possible to ignore the noise and see the larger patterns that really matter. The proverbial power of hindsight comes into play then.

Yet we are left with a difficult question: *How do you tackle the challenge of real-time learning that is both essential for the integration's success and difficult to achieve under the conditions of an integration?* Undertaking this integration-critical learning seems to pose a threat to the integration's momentum, yet that momentum depends upon the learning being achieved during the integration. Indeed, 'integration-critical learning' can be defined as 'learning that is essential for the momentum of an integration'.

> **One of the most challenging questions for today's best integrators is when and how to undertake integration-critical learning.**

To answer that question, we need to take a closer look at corporate self-knowledge – a concept that has run through each of the chapters of this book, generally in implicit form. The integration-critical learning that is most difficult often involves the acquisition or application of corporate self-knowledge.

The Role of Corporate Self-Knowledge

At the beginning of an integration, managers often feel overwhelmed by the need for learning because there are so many unknowns. Greg Hill, integration manager for Shell's 2002 acquisition of Enterprise Oil, stressed how the problem of imperfect knowledge is worst at the beginning: 'Integrations are a chaotic mess initially. That's just the nature of the beast. They're a journey of discovery. You can do your best at planning and integration, but you're going to get surprised. It's just impossible not to be, because you can't know everything there is to know.'

Suddenly you need to collaborate in the fullest possible way with the managers of another company, one whose processes, systems, and culture may differ from yours in countless ways that may remain opaque for some time. Moreover, much of what you do learn in the early stages can be disconcerting. One CEO confided to us his reaction after a close look at his new acquisition: 'Almost everything that we've uncovered has been worse than we thought it would be.'

The need to learn about your partner is so powerfully salient that it may block attention from the complementary need to learn about yourself, that is, to develop corporate self-knowledge. The latter need emerged powerfully from our research.

In our survey two traits of the *acquirer* – a culture for performance and tolerance of risk and diversity – were strong predictors of acquisition success, ranking number two and three behind the presence of post-integration learning routines.[4] That contrasted with the lack of any clear finding for attributes of the *acquired company*. This, of course, is the contrary of the common view that what matters most is what you *buy*. It turns out that who you *are* could be even more important.

These tantalizing findings underscore the importance of merger partners knowing themselves and using the integration as an opportunity to apply and build up this self-knowledge. In fact, corporate self-knowledge consistently plays a central role in healthy mergers. The following pages describe some of the many ways it plays that role, both alluding to examples given in earlier chapters and offering some fresh ones.

The Power of Corporate Self-Knowledge

Corporate self-knowledge enables you...

... to identify significant gaps in your own capabilities

... to discover where your estimates of your own capabilities are inflated or out of date

... to recognize where your understanding of your own strengths is incomplete

... to see how your normally effective habits may be counter-productive in an integration context

... to develop the humility needed to identify and make use of your partner's strengths

... to see your company as others see it

... to recognize improvement opportunities that have been there all along (i.e., 'unfreezing' opportunities)

At the most basic level, corporate self-knowledge is needed to identify gaps in your current capabilities that might hinder the integration or limit the potential of the merged company. Somewhat less obvious is the difficulty of calibrating your assessment of your capabilities to the conditions that will be faced by the newly merged company. John Watson of Chevron described how he saw this adjustment taking place – and experienced it himself:

> There were a lot of Chevron people, including myself, that felt that the combined company was just going to be a bigger Chevron. Some aspects of the merger have been hard because it took us a bit of time to realize that the larger company could not continue to do things the same way as it had in the past. That was a pretty subtle challenge on the Chevron side.

Corporate self-knowledge is not the product of a search for some intangible and elusive essence, an imaginary 'soul' of the company. It rather involves understanding yourself as a company competing with other companies to provide value to customers in a dynamic marketplace. It is deeply contextual and relative. Paradoxically, therefore, knowledge of other companies is often a catalyst for developing corporate self-knowledge. This of course is the simple insight that is at the heart of benchmarking.

To take a very concrete example: What does it mean to 'know' that you excel at logistics? A consumer goods company prided itself on its performance in this area until it discovered that the performance of its new acquisition was actually much better. It considered a crash program in this area, but in the end opted to redesign the logistics processes after the merger as part of the post-integration learning agenda.

Thus a subtle but powerful benefit of mergers is the opportunity they provide to recalibrate your assessment of your own capabilities where it may be inflated or out of date. Through the close encounter with another company a merger can enlarge your awareness of your context – in this case, of the ways similar companies run their logistics processes – and thereby sharpen your understanding of your own company.

Apparently, few companies enter the merger process with the expectation of discovering such opportunities. In our survey, standalone cost improvements realized in the *partner's* operations exceeded expectations 14 per cent of the time, while standalone cost improvements in *one's own* operations exceeded expectations 26 per cent of the time – nearly twice as often. Evidently a merger is a good forcing device for learning that one could cut costs *even without a merger*.

The attainment of corporate self-knowledge does not always involve such bracing but ultimately beneficial blows to corporate self-esteem. In fact, often the opposite happens: the integration serves as an opportunity to develop a much deeper understanding of your greatest strengths.

For example, we saw in Chapter 5 that Orange managers struggled to articulate the power of the Orange brand to their new France Telecom counterparts. This was not a peculiarity of that company, but rather a characteristic that is common to many companies that have developed particularly successful brands or business processes. Much of the knowledge involved, although very real, remains tacit until there is a need to share it with another party.

Sometimes it is clear that the encounter between managers and technologists with complementary skills could lead to important innovation that cannot be predicted with any precision. In such cases, maximizing the 'surface area'– the level of contact between the two groups – can pay off well over time. As P&G's A.G. Lafley noted:

> Gillette is a company like us built on innovation in the best of their core businesses. So I'm hopeful that we'll learn from each other. They have the mechanical engineers, and we have the chemical engineers. I'm very hopeful that this will open up new businesses to us, because when we put these two kinds of engineers together, they will see things that we don't see today because our view of the world is bounded.

Yet some important learning opportunities can be defined much more concretely, and corporate self-knowledge can help in their definition. Lafley offered an example of an important area where Gillette was ahead. 'They already have a seamless unified technical community that supports their business communities. We've been migrating there, but haven't gone all the way there yet. So we need to take a serious look at where they are.' Recognizing that your partner has made more progress against one of your high-priority goals is obviously an important discovery.

One of the more sobering realities of business is that almost any valuable management practice can actually destroy value if applied in an inappropriate context. A European transportation company prided itself on the 'just go for it' mindset of its local managers – surely a valuable trait in most business contexts. But it was self-aware enough to realize that this trait could complicate its integrations of freight forwarders. Due to the scale of these integrations and their complex systems and process dependencies, the company's managers needed to restrain their natural instinct to try to beat the integration schedule and opt instead for a slower, carefully synchronized integration. Rigorous adherence to the defined schedule was a critical success factor in this case.

In some cases a capability is so deeply embedded in the corporate culture that the company has become widely known for it externally. In such cases, external reputation serves to reinforce the importance of the capability in the company's self-image. As this may be a major advantage for the company, many CEOs encourage their companies to celebrate what the outside world regards as distinctive achievements. Yet external acknowledgement of corporate strengths could also make an integration harder in some ways that are not immediately obvious.

Greg Hill noted, for example, that Shell's culture made it somewhat more difficult to adopt the detail orientation needed to succeed with the integration of Enterprise Oil in 2002: 'Shell's heritage is that of a strategic company with big bets, big moves, scenarios, and all that. We're not about detailed work that's grinding the flour finer. But merger integration is all about grinding the flour finer.' So Hill pushed the organization against its ingrained tendencies by, for example, insisting on meticulous use of the integration templates and strict compliance with deadlines.

As we have seen, the capability that poses the greatest challenge for you may actually be a well-honed general integration approach. The story of Arrow Electronics' long-delayed integration of Anthem (at the opening of this chapter) illustrates the importance of recognizing the inapplicability of an integration approach that had proven to be highly successful in other contexts. This recognition of the limits of your strengths is an important part of corporate self-knowledge.

Increased humility is a natural outcome of the pursuit of corporate self-knowledge. As you recognize your company's weaknesses and place its strengths in context, you inevitably become more curious about the traits of your partner, and more open to the possibility of benefiting from them.

You may find this to be difficult. You may discover that your company is too rigid and arrogant to tolerate a partner's operational and cultural differences – not to speak of learning from them. On the other hand, if you are not handicapped in this way, the integration may deepen your knowledge of yourself as much as it enables you to learn about your partner.

As we heard from Peter Wuffli in Chapter 4, corporate humility was a critical factor that enabled Swiss Bank Corp (which later merged with UBS AG) to begin the transformation of its own culture through its acquisition of O'Connor & Associates in 1992. Perhaps the most important lesson for SBC in that experience was that its own aspirations had been needlessly limited by its self-image as a conventional Swiss bank. Wuffli articulated well how transformational corporate self-knowledge can be for a large acquirer:

> The O'Connor partners set in motion a cultural revolution by helping to foster a world-class ambition. The traditional Swiss way had been for the three big banks to compare their balance sheets, growth and net profits, but these young O'Connor guys had no respect for hierarchy or historical legacies. They just kept asking 'Who is the best in the industry and what does it take to compete with them?' When we told them UBS was an important competitor in Switzerland, they then said, 'Okay, but you have to compare yourselves to the best worldwide.' And that eventually became the ambition of the entire senior management of the bank.

O'Connor's managers were unusually self-confident. However, when you are in the role of acquirer, the acquired company's managers may instead be deferential and thus make it harder for you to be humble.

Alcan's Dick Evans discovered this during the 2000 integration of Algroup. He recalled that the attitude of the Algroup managers was 'Hey, you acquired us. Just tell me what to do. I want to do what you want and I want to succeed. Give me some reasonable direction and if I think you're totally unreasonable I'll push back, but just tell me.' Some of Alcan's managers considered this attitude to be appropriate.

At the time, however, Alcan needed to address deficiencies in its own management systems, so it definitely did not have all the answers. Evans was therefore determined not to play the know-it-all role of the classic acquirer: 'There were awkward moments where we had to openly debate what the right thing to do was in this case or that case' he recalled. 'And managing the inclination of the Alcan people to impose something worse or not as good as something that Algroup had was *the* challenge of the integration. We also had to continue to stress to the Algroup people that they had a voice.'

The business press often demonizes the managers of acquirers for their arrogance, but the onus for achieving a healthy merger that draws upon the strengths of both sides is not entirely on them. The managers of the acquired company must also have the pride and self-confidence to move past thinking of themselves – as Kevin Sharer put it – as 'conquered'.

Yet to help them move past this, the managers of the acquirer need to be able to see their own company as the acquired company's managers do. Corporate self-knowledge thus means more than knowing who *you* are. It also means knowing who you are *for others*. Amgen's managers, for example, might be inclined to think of their company as a surging biotech upstart instead of a large pharma company, but as Sharer noted in Chapter 4, the managers of their acquisition could hardly be expected to look upon Amgen in that way: 'As far as the guys from Immunex are concerned, we *are* a pharma giant.'

David Shedlarz of Pfizer – which indisputably is a pharma giant – made a complementary point. You have no grounds for assuming that the managers of your acquisition will share your strategic perspective:

> It would be desirable to have the strategic way forward shared by the target company's management up front, but in many respects that might just not be possible. For instance, if Pfizer is going to play scale, and in a number of areas already owns a large share of the marketplace, our perceptions are going to be quite different from those of someone who has a much more modest market share.

As with any company, Pfizer's strategic perspective is the outcome of an extended process not just of strategizing but also of competing day-to-day in the marketplace. In the language of Chapter 3, your specific 'backstory' strongly affects how you look at the world. One important element of corporate self-knowledge is therefore the recognition that although your merger partners can and do share the merged company's future with you, they cannot share your backstory in the full sense. Managers from both sides of the merger boundary will of course slowly develop a shared backstory as the merged company progresses, but this will not happen immediately.

Even if you are the acquirer and have a strong performance history, the acquired company's managers might not automatically defer to your judgment about key integration decisions. After all, they have critical knowledge about their company that you do not possess, and they might be top performers in their own right.

Large serial acquirers with a strong track record should be particularly wary of assuming that they know upfront the best way to improve a high-performing acquisition. In fact, formal research shows that merger contexts are particularly prone to so-called 'superstitious learning', a condition in which the subjective feeling of having merger capabilities is compelling but the actual understanding of what works, what does not work, and why, is flawed. Furthermore, this problem seems to grow as acquisition experience accumulates, and to subside only with significant investments in articulating and codifying what has been learned.[5]

In reflecting on Wachovia's 2004 integration of SouthTrust, Steve Boehm stressed the importance of respecting what the acquisition brings to the table:

> However good the leadership team at Wachovia may be, it has not run SouthTrust for the last 15 or 20 years – a period when they've experienced an incredible run. Of course we're still interested in applying those things that we think we know a lot about that could help make their business even more successful going forward. But the only way to do that is to have key leaders from their organization integrally involved in developing the business plans.

Given SouthTrust's 'backstory' with its theme of consistently strong performance, its managers naturally see their Wachovia colleagues as partners rather than as tutors.

During the course of an integration you will find yourself adopting disciplines, mechanisms and cultural traits on a project basis that would serve you well in continuous use after the merger. This is a common effect of the integration period: in scrambling to get things done under pressure you may discover better ways to manage.

One integration manager confided to us that an integration had a tonic effect on the weak sense of accountability in the acquirer's culture. In the past, the culture was rather relaxed. Trying one's best had been considered enough, even when the results fell below expectations. The public synergy commitments changed that:

> When people come up short on delivering, then they are still accountable for what they signed up for because we've gone to the street with that expectation. So we have to go back and find other ways to close the gap. The detailed planning, the documentation, the target setting, the tracking to hold people accountable for results – those are capabilities that have come with the integration. And at least some degree we have applied them across the business.

Such an across-the-board toughening of the accountability culture is perhaps the most common intangible benefit of the integration process, and it usually involves changes to formal management systems and processes.

Sometimes the integration experience leads managers to recalibrate systems and processes that are functional but could be improved. For example, Steve Boehm told us that Wachovia developed 'readiness assessment reviews' as part of the integration process and then found that they could be productively applied to all major change events in the bank. The reviews enabled the integration team to assess the full set of impacts of any proposed change, both within the company and beyond. Institutionalization of this level of analysis enabled Wachovia to make all its change processes healthier, not just its mergers.

David Shedlarz noted that before the acquisition of Warner-Lambert in 2000 and the merger with Pharmacia in 2003, Pfizer managers had a penchant for rather formal and deliberate decision-making based on vigorous debate of multiple options. The emphasis was very much on making sure that the decision was the right one before proceeding. During an integration, however, managers need to make tough calls quickly. They must learn to accept that some of them will need to be reversed. Reflection on the contrast between the two decision-making approaches led to a recognition of some of the problems with the more formal approach. So ultimately Pfizer recalibrated:

> During these two integrations some of us began to question the old deliberateness, whose drawback is that in some cases you don't take action until it's too late. Moreover, you are less likely to admit to yourself that you've chosen the wrong course of action and correct the way you're doing things. So in the last two years we've found a different balance in terms of how far we'll take the analysis before we act. It's earlier than we chose to do in the past.

Of course, you could just *tell* your managers to make faster decisions at any time, and many CEOs do just that. However, such exhortations often do not change much. A company's decision-making routines are actually quite complex and depend upon a shared tacit understanding of when an issue is ripe for decision. Any significant acceleration requires the kind of bold experimentation that can make managers acutely uncomfortable. An integration effectively forces the managers to experiment because there is no other way to achieve the deliverables. Comparison of the outcomes of these alternative paces typically does not lead to wholesale adoption of the integration's decision-making pace, but rather to a new rhythm that lies somewhere between them.

The experience of an integration may also lead you to adopt formal mechanisms for ongoing use. John Watson of Chevron described how the role of the integration steering committee for the merger was expanded to cover routine performance management: 'Our Decision Review Board will continue to do whatever is necessary about outstanding integration matters, but it will also look at the SBUs' businesses overall. That's pretty high praise for a process that's a centralized activity in a very decentralized company.' Shedlarz noted, by contrast, that Pfizer decided to decentralize some decisions that, in the light of their integration experience, were no longer seen as a good use of senior managers' time.

From a long-term perspective, all companies tend to move back and forth along the spectrum from centralization to decentralization because new times bring new challenges and a need to adjust. An integration provides an opportunity to move along this spectrum on a project basis. In effect, it serves as a pilot of an alternative way of managing. In this case, corporate self-knowledge takes the form of a realistic appraisal of the strengths and weaknesses of the company's managerial norms. Of course a sense of any difficulties involved in moving the organization closer to the piloted alternative is also needed.

So we believe that a merger provides unique opportunities for a company to come to know itself better and to apply that knowledge productively. To be sure, as the examples in this section suggest, not all the opportunities that are discovered will be strictly integration-critical. Yet they almost all pay off sooner or later. One hallmark of a healthy merger, therefore, is that a *wiser* company emerges from it.

Some Common Principles

The codification of integration lessons learned has advanced significantly over the years not just because the payback is substantial but also because this process lends itself to continuous improvement. Almost all companies that make a serious effort improve in this area after multiple rounds of integration.

Integration-critical learning is much harder to master because it takes such different forms from one merger to the next. We have selected a diverse range of examples for this chapter, but cannot claim to have covered the map. A learning challenge that could make or break your next merger may be completely different from any that you have faced before or any that we have illustrated here.

However, there are some important recurrent patterns. We offer three practical principles that can make this slippery challenge somewhat easier to manage.

■ **Take personal responsibility for the tough calls on momentum and learning**. As we have seen, the default behavior for most integration teams is to maximize momentum at the expense of learning. If you do not actively advocate integration-critical learning, you can hardly expect those who are preoccupied with synergy targets and milestones to do so. In some modern manufacturing plants, every worker is empowered to stop the assembly line if he discovers a problem that could compromise the quality of what is being built. Integration teams do not work that way because the pressure on them to keep up the pace is simply too great.

The need for senior leadership is particularly acute where there is a transformational aspiration and the demand for learning is correspondingly high. When Australia's Suncorp-Metway acquired the GIO, AMP's general insurance unit, in 2001, the company initially promised A$80 million in synergies to the market. After three months they announced that they had captured A$160 million, and after another year, they upped their target to A$400 million.

The financial analysts failed to anticipate the scale of the value-creation. They looked narrowly at GIO's costs and asked what bringing these costs down to industry-standard levels could yield. Yet Suncorp-Metway MD Steve Jones and his managers were looking at the merger as a catalyst for transforming their own operations in such areas as wealth management and banking operations. So, for example, after noting the strong similarities in risk assessment between the general insurance operations of their acquisition and their own retail lending and credit card operations, they decided to move to a new business model at the back end based on a unified operations center.

Clearly such a daunting learning challenge cannot be met unless the senior managers are very committed sponsors of it. Yet the same holds for less dramatic learning challenges, particularly if there is a need to fill a gap in corporate self-knowledge. In fact, sometimes integration-critical learning will appear downright prosaic, as when Chevron's managers learned that ChevronTexaco (as the merged company was initially called) could not be just 'a bigger Chevron'. Active leadership is required to meet such challenges because they are often seen as serious enough by the people involved to pose a serious risk to the integration.

- **Ensure that intensive learning takes place in the top team early on**. Major mergers always a significant learning burden on the senior leaders. In fact, the first leadership challenge – creating the new company at the top before the close – is as much a learning challenge as anything else.

  This is yet another case where thinking in terms of a trade-off between momentum and learning can be counterproductive. The intensive learning that is taking place on the top team in the first few weeks might be interpreted by outsiders and even by some on the team as a loss of momentum.

  It may in fact simply reflect the natural rhythm of team building in the early weeks. At first, there is a flurry of activity as the newly announced senior managers take early steps to protect the merger's health (for example, communicating with customers and employees) and make key set-up decisions to prepare for the integration (for example, appointing the integration manager and key integration team leaders). This is followed by a period of intense interaction within the team as its members learn about each other's companies.

  This is multilayered learning: they are not just aiming to find out 'Who are your customers?' and 'What are your costs' but also 'Who are *you*?', 'How can we get things done together?' and even (as we have seen in this chapter) 'Who are *we*?' In a healthy merger, the new company emerges first in the top team during this intensive learning period. There then follows another flurry of activity as the formal integration gets underway.

  Even though this is the round of learning that is most critical for the merger's momentum, it can be taken too far. It should be intensive, but not protracted. It should result in a high-performing team – not a self-conscious talking shop.

- **Institutionalize learning by heavily involving the line**. Maximizing line ownership is of course widely-accepted integration practice. But sometimes this only means that targets and processes are transferred from the integration team to the line. Such handoffs may cause a loss of momentum at the integration's close. The ownership must be richer and more deeply embedded in the line than any such handoff could achieve. For David Shedlarz ownership meant engaging with line managers when the integration process was still in its formative stages, and then allowing them to help shape it. 'We made sure they bought into the process by jointly developing it with them. We didn't hand them a form and say, "Please fill that out." They were involved from the very beginning in terms of developing the templates, reflecting on the past experience, and further perfecting the process.'

Like everyone else, managers feel much stronger ownership of what they have taught themselves to do than of what they have been taught by others to do. Broader involvement of managers in the learning process is yet another example where momentum and learning appear to be in conflict but are actually mutually dependent.

As we have seen, not all the valuable learning opportunities that arise from a merger can be fully exploited during the integration period. Some learning activity will continue well past the project's end, and some cannot be practically taken up until later.

Dick Evans of Alcan argued strongly for shutting down the integration team as early as possible because this helps to shift the burden for shaping the longer-term learning agenda from the integration team to the line:

> Suppose for example that the Primary Metal group decides that it's not going to redesign its whole IT system during the integration but tables that for future consideration. The fact that line managers have made the decision means that the idea will not drop off the list. But if the integration team works on it, then the idea may be lost when the team disbands – even if it's a good one. And even if it's not lost the line managers will have to learn about it all over again.

Momentum and learning depend critically upon continuity of involvement. This is such an important principle that it led Jean-François Pontal of Orange to create some new line positions in order to maintain important learning initiatives after the integration was ended. That is a creative way to avoid a disruptive hand-off, but in most cases the simpler solution – involving the line in the learning from the beginning – works just fine.

CHAPTER 7

Mastering the Language of Integration

Senior managers need to define a value-added leadership role for themselves based on a creative and expansive understanding of how the merger affects the corporation. As their integration teams become more proficient and their integration tools and techniques more deeply institutionalized, senior managers' charge is to resist the emergence of complacency. They must strive for a truly healthy merger. The preceding five chapters on the leadership challenges have provided a view of what this leadership entails – a view grounded in actual leadership experience from many integrations in a diverse set of companies.

Unfortunately, any leadership book presents a rather stylized picture of how leadership actually works. Space constraints and the need to maintain a rapid pace dictate this. The emphasis here is squarely on striking insights, decisions and actions – as if these made all the difference. Based on these high points of the story, it is up to the reader to imagine what actually happened in hundreds or thousands of day-to-day leadership interactions over the course of the integration.

Merger veterans know how misleading stylized accounts of merger leadership can be. The big ideas, bold themes, and pivotal moments have their considerable effect precisely because they are reinforced by numerous non-dramatic leadership interventions. These countless 'leadership nudges' receive little attention in leadership books.

This familiar point always holds true of leadership, but is particularly salient during a merger. When doing project work, managers cannot readily turn to the deeply-grooved routines that make them efficient in their regular jobs. Moreover, integrations are especially intensive projects, where the temptation to stay in 'execution mode' can be overwhelming. Reflective managers regularly complain that integration work leaves them no time to think.

Notwithstanding the need for execution, far more is at stake than just defined project deliverables. A merger is a disruptive event that can have a host of positive or negative, concrete or intangible, predictable or surprising effects on the health of the new company. Thus we have the worst of all worlds: a period where highly reflective management is urgently needed but especially difficult to provide. This is the dilemma that the members of your integration team find themselves in.

> **Your integration team members urgently need to step back from the integration but are singularly hard pressed to do so.**

The language introduced in this book – for example, the top team as the 'ultimate integration template', the 'corporate story', the 'performance culture' and 'performance contract', 'integration-critical learning', 'corporate self-knowledge' – is intended to redirect your attention from the nuts and bolts realities of the integration team's work to the larger implications of the integration for corporate health. The oddity of some of this language is intended to help you break out of the project mindset. So, for example, as culture has become familiar in the integration literature as an impediment to merger goals we have reframed the discussion by offering the positive yet paradoxical concept of a 'performance culture'. Similarly, as highly-polished merger communications sometimes leave managers and employees confused about how the merger fits in, we introduce the concept of the 'corporate story' to highlight your responsibility for providing the essential context for the merger. Yet this is *not* the language of integration. It is too far abstracted from the concrete realities of project work. It is also not the language that effective merger leaders generally adopt – as a scan of quotations in this book will quickly reveal.

You may well be privileged to have on your integration team people whose insights into some aspects of corporate health may be much deeper than yours. You might have, for example, someone who better understands what motivates the sales force than anyone on the top team. Your diagnosis of what is needed to achieve a healthy merger will depend upon fruitful dialogue with such people, and also with others outside the project or even outside the company.

Nevertheless, the ultimate responsibility for translating your plan for achieving a healthy merger into 'executable' language must remain yours. Merger leaders who limit their role to the crafting of visionary language run a serious risk of having nothing emerge from the integration that remotely resembles their vision. Indeed, they are not even in a position to claim that their vision is feasible. The simplistic notion that the leader's role is to think grand thoughts and the follower's role is to translate them into action has had disastrous consequences in business generally and in mergers in particular. In fact, one of the more sobering implications from the discussion of the last five chapters is that the translation of sound insights about corporate health into a practical program of integration work is a task that you cannot afford to delegate away, even after what may appear to be a strong start for the integration. Merger leaders must stay engaged for an extended period and provide a continuous series of leadership nudges.

A Different Starting Point

In earlier chapters we stressed the *differentiation* of the senior merger leadership role. To add value you must *not* think of yourself as a sort of senior integration manager. In this chapter, however, we shift gears and stress the importance of adopting the perspective of the integration manager and team. Just as you rely on them to deliver the healthy merger that you envisage, they rely on you to help them by speaking the language of integration. Although your role is differentiated, the language you use must be broadly accessible.

If this book had been written for members of the integration team, we would have begun very differently. Rather than start with the metaphor of corporate health as a forcing device for enlarging aspirations, we would have started with the familiar realities of integration project work. In other words, rather than working 'outside-in' from the extremely broad concept of corporate health to the detailed world of the integration project we would have proceeded 'inside-out'. This would mean beginning with integration project realities and incrementally broadening the perspective until the corporate health implications of the merger clearly emerged. Whereas the outside-in argument is helpful with the sweeping, open-ended diagnosis that is central to your role, the inside-out perspective is superior for enabling integration team members to execute in a way that increases the chances of achieving a healthy merger.

The key here is that integration team members naturally want to begin with what has been proven to work on integrations. They will have little trouble grasping the general idea that mergers need to be 'healthier', but they will naturally seek to interpret that aspiration in terms of how they should adapt what they are already doing. After all, unlike senior merger leaders, they are starting from a very well-defined idea of what their roles are.

> **You may need to create a leadership role for yourself from a clean slate, but your integration team members already have well-defined roles that they will assume as a starting point.**

Learning to speak the language of integration therefore involves routinely starting from – or at least connecting with – what integration team members rightly consider to be the primary principles of their work. These are the three classic lessons on how to integrate companies, and they would provide the main content of a book written for the integration team.

As your ability to communicate effectively with the integration team boils down to a ready command of these lessons, in the following few pages we summarize what a book written for the integration team would cover.

Even by the standards of managerial writing, the literature on merger integration tends to be highly prescriptive. It converges around a set of defined rules that are offered as best practice for integrating two companies. On closer inspection, however, it becomes clear that the application of many of these rules is highly contingent on the context, and there is substantial variation in their use. For all that, we can speak of a broad consensus in how to manage merger integrations.

At one level, the integration literature consists of a prodigious mountain of process rules for – among other things – setting up an integration office, identifying and capturing synergies, communicating to stakeholders, protecting the base business, consolidating processes, locations and positions, managing cultural change, maintaining integration momentum, and preparing for new post-integration value-creation opportunities. Some of its domains involve specialists, for example, in technology and engineering; in financial and management accounting; in the optimization of networks of locations and staff; or in the applicable laws in multiple jurisdictions for such areas as employment, supplier contracts, leases, and the sharing of information during the pre-close period. Above all else, the merger challenge is an integrated one: Everything is connected to everything else at one or more removes, and the project dependencies are seemingly endless. Thus the integration literature can be seen as an exhaustive enumeration of things to do – and not do – to deliver a desired project outcome in a coherent way. For all but the few companies that manage vast, multi-year projects (for example, aerospace companies), this is likely to be the most complex project check-list they will ever need to use.

However, there is a simpler way to think about this sprawling body of writing. Managers, consultants and researchers have developed it over the years in response to recurrent major integration challenges. What are the hard-won lessons that have shaped its development?

Three such classic lessons tower over others in terms of their general importance:

- *Focus tenaciously on value*
- *Systematically address people issues*
- *Dynamically tailor each integration*

'Value', 'people' and 'tailoring' capture the three grand principles of the integration literature.

> **The integration experience of thousands of managers over several decades can be boiled down to value, people and tailoring.**

Behind each of these lessons there is a substantial body of managerial writing. In addition, some elements of these lessons have been subjected to intensive academic research. Managers who explore the managerial literature on mergers, engage consultants, or speak to peers with significant integration experience, will hear these lessons repeated again and again in various formulations.

First classic lesson: focus tenaciously on value. *A generation ago, it was widely thought that value creation was primarily the concern of the strategists who plan the company's M&A initiatives and of the negotiating team that strikes the deals. The integration team's challenge was seen as implementation of the project that followed the value creation. Those days are long gone.[1]*

In fact, these days the dealmakers are more likely to be blamed for locking in value destruction through excessive premiums than they are to be praised for locking in value creation just by doing the deal. Yet even for properly priced mergers, there is much work to be done in identifying and capturing value after the agreement is struck. The rough estimates of synergies must be quickly translated into specific value opportunities that the integration team and line managers can go after.[2]

It is usually not so difficult to maintain the focus on value during the early weeks of hectic spreadsheet analysis. Often there is a sense of exhilaration at this stage, particularly if the total value of synergies identified shoots past the overall target promised to the markets. However, the hardest part is yet to come.[3] That exciting synergy total may be vulnerable to a number of risks. Most obviously, some of the estimates may turn out to be wrong. The cost of capturing the synergies may balloon beyond what is expected. Line managers may challenge the synergies that they are expected to achieve as unrealistic. Value may also be destroyed in any number of ways, for example, through the loss of talent and customers due to neglect[4] or through a reduction in technological capability caused by poor integration decisions.[5] An important trade-off in objectives, such as that between cost reduction through consolidation of facilities and revenue protection through maintenance of levels of customer service, may not be fully understood. Trade-offs in the integration process itself with numerous implications for value creation, such as that between speed in decision-making and speed in implementation,[6] may receive little attention. Similarly, unexpected opportunities to drive the synergy total higher may be overlooked or filed away for adoption in a future that never arrives.

Almost invariably there is a stage where the long hours and sheer detail complexity of the integration threatens to trigger a change in the focus from finding and capturing value to simply making it through the process. This unspoken shift to lower aspirations for value creation is particularly likely to occur at the moment when the true scale of the process management challenge dawns on everyone.

Generally the process burden takes its toll on the team. It can therefore become extremely challenging to maintain the focus on value throughout an integration. It can also be hard to convey to those who have never worked on an integration or similar project why this is not as straightforward as it sounds. 'Focus tenaciously on value' is such an obviously sensible prescription that the difficulty of doing so can be all too easily underestimated.

To maintain this focus, it is not enough to monitor the synergy total on the integration team's dashboard. Paradoxically, focus actually requires a broader view. Managers must look beyond the synergy numbers to the entire process through which they are identified and captured, and beyond the organizational areas that are being directly integrated to the entire corporate system including customers and other external stakeholders. Developing early on such a comprehensive understanding of the full value creation challenge does not reduce the importance of the synergy target, but rather places it in a richer context where it can be more effectively managed.

There is also a tough-minded business calculation behind this rather expansive and imaginative view of value creation. Forms of value that are much less obvious than standard cost efficiencies and cross-selling benefits are more 'capturable', that is, less likely to be ceded to the seller at the negotiating table through a higher acquisition premium. The more subtle forms of value involve factors over which the sellers cannot knowledgeably and credibly negotiate. The potential of the integration to 'unfreeze' your organization's unproductive practices is a common example. At a more creative level, you might have special insight into how the merger could catalyze new service initiatives that you are considering. In general, no external observer is as well-placed as you are to assess the options that a merger opens up. Creating value beyond the premium paid often depends upon identifying opportunities across the two companies, not just in the parts where synergistic benefits are clearly definable.

The discovery that value takes many forms and must be managed in such a comprehensive and rigorous way has had numerous effects. The structure, roles and processes of today's integration projects reflect this matured understanding of the challenge of identifying and capturing value. For example, in most projects functions that are crucial for longer-term value creation such as branding, supplier management and R&D have much stronger representation on the integration team than was common in the past. Moreover, there are often revenue teams in place to identify and document opportunities that may be pursued immediately or deferred until after the integration is complete.

Second classic lesson: systematically address people issues. *Whereas integration novices may be taken aback by the difficulty of focusing on value, they are often generally aware of the havoc that unaddressed people issues can play with an integration. Significant time spent in any large organization will provide many opportunities to observe how dependent performance is on engaging the full commitment and competence of managers and employees. Given the shock that a major merger provides to the two companies involved, it is clear that significant people issues may arise. On top of everything else, the business press often dramatizes stories of troubled mergers by emphasizing the people issues – sometimes to the neglect of more prosaic problems like unrealistic synergy expectations.[7]*

Because of its project complexity, some integration managers have a tendency to see the integration challenge as a kind of engineering problem. If this leads them to ignore the people issues as irrelevant to the integration 'machine', the consequences can be severe.

However, the engineer's mental habit of tackling problems from a systems perspective can be helpful provided that people are considered an integral part of that system. The decisive point in this second classic lesson is the recognition that people issues can and must be approached systematically. Managers have learned over the years that there is no need to be blindsided by the predictable people issues. It is now standard practice among superior integrators, for example, to be fully ready for intensive communications to all stakeholder groups at the point of announcement.

Perhaps the most dramatic people issue is a confrontation between individuals on the top team who hold conspicuously different views of the future of the merged company. Yet many other people issues can occur anywhere in the organization down to the front line, as well as beyond the corporate boundary. Your most serious people issue might not involve employees, financial analysts or customers at all – the usual suspects – but rather a business partner that wants to reassess his or her relationship with you. A manufacturer may find, for example, that some of the company's distributors are reluctant to carry the full retail product line of the merged company. External people issues need to be addressed as systematically as internal ones.

The largest-scale people issue in integrations is that between two whole peoples, that is, cultural incompatibility between the two companies. A common version of this problem occurs when a large company buys a smaller one largely for the sake of cultural characteristics (for example, entrepreneurialism, technological innovativeness) that it does not itself possess. Here again it is surprising how many companies take few steps to prepare for this challenge even though much has been learned in recent years about how to shelter an acquisition from too much influence from its new parent. A merger of equals, by contrast, may be defined as one where the people issue of achieving a fair balance between the two sides' personnel, processes, systems and so forth is central to its success – although 'fair' may be interpreted variously either as 'equitable' or as 'merit-based'.

People issues of course can be difficult to address because the integration involves change that at least some people are bound to experience negatively – even if there are no job losses. Moreover, their reactions to the integration are not fully predictable, in part because they are hearing interpretations of the merger from non-official sources, such as colleagues and the press. A systematic approach to people issues therefore provides no guarantee of a successful outcome. It does, however, improve your odds of managing them.[8]

The better integrators continuously enrich their understanding of this classic lesson. In particular, they are extending its application well beyond the managers and employees whose people issues were the first to receive close attention. Some companies today are almost as systematic in managing their customers' experience of the merged company as they are in integrating the two organizations. However, few companies exhibit similar sophistication in their approach to other key stakeholder groups such as business partners, communities and regulators.

Third classic lesson: dynamically tailor each integration. *The first two classic lessons effectively combine to generate a third. Tailoring is necessary primarily because mergers differ so much in terms of the specific ways in which value is created (and protected) and in terms of the specific people issues that are salient.*

The underlying value logic can vary greatly from one merger to the next. In the broadest sense, 'synergy' is a term of art that covers such diverse benefits as cost savings through consolidation of activities, the strengthening of customer offerings through complementary product and service lines, the acquisition of business or technical skills, the leveraging of a partner's market access, customer base or brand, and the reinvigoration of a large acquirer by means of the entrepreneurial energy of the acquired company. The merger may even be a forcing device for transforming performance beyond the level of either predecessor company.

Similarly, the combination may trigger any of a number of people issues, both within the merging company's boundary and beyond it. The most critical people issues that are encountered generally mirror the value logic closely. If you are acquiring a smaller company for the strength of its brands and customer relationships, for example, you must take steps to protect both, and also deal effectively with the managers and employees of the acquisition that have made key contributions to its strength in the marketplace.

From a very early stage, researchers and consultants have developed merger typologies to reduce the bewildering variety of mergers to a handful of standard types that can be managed in predictable ways. The types are largely based on the value logic and the relevant people issues. A roll-up integration, for example, is advised where the central goal is to save costs through consolidation. Its human resource processes are naturally designed to deal with extensive layoffs. A 'keep separate' approach which limits the extent not only of integration but also of information flows may be preferable where it is important to preserve the motivation and the creative spirit of highly talented people. A merger in which two technology companies combine to achieve complementarity in their R&D programs is different again. Its success fundamentally depends upon their ability to share knowledge and processes in order to co-develop new insights.[9]

Some acquirers specialize in a particular type of acquisition and therefore use the same integration approach over and over. There is a danger here: they may develop such a sophisticated way of tackling the value and people challenges over a series of uniform (usually small) acquisitions that they fail to notice what is crucially different in a new case. What happens then is that the 'value, people, tailoring' wisdom becomes ossified as a routine integration approach: 'This is where we make money, these are the people issues we always see, and here's the integration formula that always works for us.'

At the extreme, some managers implicitly assume that what has worked for them in an initial integration will work in all subsequent ones. 'Tailor once, repeat forever': that formula is likely to lead sooner or later to a negative surprise. Yet even the company that has refined its integration approach over multiple integrations may be vulnerable. Perhaps the most common reason why experienced acquirers occasionally stumble badly with an integration is that they become overconfident about their well-honed routines. As a result, they fail to recognize what is importantly different about the current integration.[10]

Most of the tough integration calls involve tailoring around the relationship between value and people issues in some way. For example, a major unfreezing opportunity may be unrealizable unless you are willing to take on entrenched resistance from some powerful players. The impact on productivity of alternative ways of combining the R&D functions of the two companies may depend on subtle human factors. The pace at which you can reasonably move with the integration depends in part on the ability of managers and employees to learn and adapt to the value objectives of the merger.

Unfortunately, intimately linking the value focus to people issues runs against a generation of integration practice that has led to ever more specialized roles. On most integration teams it is easy to distinguish those team members whose attention is centered on the synergy numbers from those who are concerned with issues with employees, customers and other stakeholder groups. This bifurcation has emerged because the mindset and skills required are very different. For the most part, this is a positive development: Integration teams run more smoothly because of this specialization. However, it has also sharpened the need for the integrate team to – in effect – integrate its own work.

Moreover, tailoring is a continuing challenge throughout most integrations. Detailed planning before the close is essential, but along the way you will encounter surprises that will require you to tailor dynamically. When trying to keep an acquisition separate, for example, you will often find that the mechanisms you start with need to be calibrated. Perhaps the corporate HR processes are too intrusive, whereas there is too little interaction between the two R&D groups across the merger boundary. In other cases, a need for tailoring may be overlooked altogether during planning. For example, you may hear from business partners that they have specific concerns about the merger that you did not anticipate.

Mastering the Language of Integration

Although this summary of what a book for the integration team might contain is only 5 per cent of the length of this volume, it touches upon many of the points made elsewhere and could be expanded to touch upon them all. We do not need to mention directly corporate health or the five leadership challenges: Virtually any idea you might want to adopt from the other chapters can be expressed in straightforward value, people and tailoring language.

Fashioning language that your people can put to use is a central part of leadership, and the range of styles that actual leaders can successfully employ is remarkable. Consider, for example, the broad range of voices captured in the pages of this book. They share a concrete vividness and relevance for their

audiences, but they also reflect the personality and enthusiasms of the individual leader.

Your *style* must remain your own. Our concern here is simply to suggest
means of translating the *content* of this book into a form that is useful to
your integration team in the context of a specific merger.

There are many ways to do this. Here we recommend three techniques
that are all based on the value, people, tailoring lessons that are so relevant
to your integration team.

- **Use questioning around the three lessons to foster thoughtfulness
  around corporate health**. Broadly speaking (1) value-creation or protection is the objective of any merger, (2) people issues of various kinds
  present the trickiest constraints on that objective, and (3) tailoring is the
  means of reconciling the value objective with the people issues. That
  simple value, people and tailoring dynamic can be used to explore
  every difficult challenge the integration team faces.

  'How is value at stake in what we are discussing?' 'What are the
  people issues?' 'How should we tailor our approach to capture or protect the value while dealing with the people issues?' Asking the first
  question can help keep your integration team from getting bogged down
  in process bureaucracy. The second reduces the risk of being blindsided
  by a people issue (for example resistance to an integration decision
  from an unexpected quarter). The third fosters creativity around a solution that nevertheless builds on experience.

  Consider, for example, Steve Boehm's reflections on the decline of
  the 'big-bang' integration model at retail banks in the US (see the
  beginning of Chapter 5). The ways in which a rapid, all-at-once conversion of process and systems could contribute to value had long been
  obvious. For years the implications of customer dissatisfaction were
  less clearly seen, and some banks evidently saw this as a temporary people issue rather than as a serious threat to value. It is only when banks
  recognized the degree to which this people issue can impact value that
  they were willing to go to the substantial effort of tailoring a conversion
  approach that introduces some delay and extra process complexity in
  exchange for higher customer satisfaction.

  In practice, the sequence of the questions may sometimes be different.
  You may, for example, identify a people issue, and then explore its implications for value. The key here is to ensure that the interrelationship
  between value and people issues is analysed in depth. This of course
  amounts to a means of diagnosing the corporate health implications of

the integration – whether or not you specifically refer to the metaphor of corporate health.

- **Crystallize and communicate one or a few specific 'health goals'.** If you spend an afternoon with the integration team noting every conceivable way in which your merger may be more or less healthy, you will run out of flip-chart paper long before the ideas stop coming. This is like one of those risk management diagnostics that produces a list of risks that is too long for managers to even take in, not to speak of managing.

In general, however, during an integration one or a few ways in which value and people issues interrelate will be of special importance. Kevin Sharer of Amgen, for example, recognized that the trauma of a lost corporate identity could adversely affect the motivation of his new managers from Immunex. Dick Evans of Alcan saw that a lack of clarify around roles and direction at the top team level could lead to a raft of poor compromises. Both these leaders took a cue from what had not worked well in a previous integration and successfully developed a 'health goal' to prevent a recurrence.

The attainment of a health goal sharply improves the chances of achieving a healthy merger. We have seen many examples of this: Michael Kay of Sky Chefs insisting that Caterair managers must meet the transformational challenge but balancing that with coaching support and the promise of a fair shot at jobs; Peter Wuffli of UBS highlighting the importance of preserving the unique contributions of each merger partner; Steve Kaufman of Arrow Electronics hitting the road to tell Anthem Electronics managers that 'separate is good'; Eric Benhamous of 3Com drawing attention again and again to the 'small things' that are crucial for talent retention and for the preservation of customer relationships; Steve Jones of Suncorp-Metway pushing his team to treat the acquisition as a new chapter in an ongoing transformation program; and so on.

It is, in fact, for practical purposes impossible to define what a perfectly healthy merger would look like. The enumeration of relevant factors would simply never end. Yet it *is* possible to define in a sentence or two what would make a given merger much healthier. The health goal is not about an illusory ideal standard, but rather about the difference between merely good and much better.

Over the course of an integration you are likely to make a large number of leadership interventions, and this may lead to some confusion as to what is really important. If you crisply articulate one or a few health goals, and repeatedly show how individual decisions and actions relate to them, your integration team will quickly recognize your priorities and follow them.

- **Use your corporate story to put the three classic lessons in context.**
On the surface the corporate story is all about connecting to people – all those stakeholders that you need to engage in one way or another. Look more closely and you will find that the corporate story also has a powerful role to play in putting the classic lessons in a larger context.

The corporate story is an articulation of how the company creates value for *others*. For each stakeholder group it answers the question 'Why are they involved with this company?' They work for it, buy from it, partner with it, invest in it and so on for identifiable reasons. It creates value as an economic entity only insofar as it provides value to them. It can have no story unless they are a part of it.

That is why exploring the corporate story with your integration team can be so useful during an integration. It can help you to identify numerous ways in which value and people issues interrelate, including some that are not obvious. The secret here is to think about value in the many forms it takes for your stakeholders.

Consider, for example, the M&A strand of your corporate story. How have the M&A challenges your company has faced shaped your story? Arrow Electronics' Steve Kaufman noted that his company's integration approach has been strongly affected by its need to secure relationships with each acquisition:

> All we're buying is relationships with customers and suppliers. That's what makes the people side of the equation so important. I'm not sure we'd have to be as people-oriented as we have forced ourselves to be if we were just after the assets. So our integration approach is tailored to the context we find ourselves in. I might come out with different answers if we were acquiring steel mills, where you don't want the people – all you want is the mill.

Others working in the industry will develop over time a sense of your corporate story. This will happen whether or not you make an effort to communicate it directly to them. Your story is revealed in the pattern of actions that you take.

Arrow's pragmatic focus on ensuring that integrations work out well for its acquisitions' managers has built up a crucial intangible asset: The reputation of being a good acquirer. This pays off in very tangible ways. As Kaufman noted, widespread familiarity with Arrow's story helped to clinch deals and to protect the value of those deals during the integration:

> If you have to get bought, you want Arrow to do the buying. That is important for any target CEO that cares about his people. What's more, on the day of the announcement, the reaction of their people is much better, so we retain more of them and capture more sales synergies. Everybody in the industry knows they get straight answers from us, and they've got an even shot at any job, even if they're from the target.

A corporate story that is attractive to managers of potential targets can boost your odds of achieving a healthy merger. Moreover, there is more involved than just the way you treat people. Also relevant, for example, is the quality of the future that is captured in your corporate story. As we saw in the UBS case, a compelling strategy is another element in the corporate story that can make mergers healthier. It pays, therefore, to ask some probing questions about what it is like for others to be drawn into your corporate story through a merger.

There is, of course, much more to your corporate story than M&A activities. For example, what operational capabilities does your company have that might play a major positive role during the integration? Events may trigger some surprising opportunities here.

The Amgen acquisition of Immunex in 2002 provides an interesting example of this. As the negotiations were underway, Immunex had just begun test production runs for a new facility in Rhode Island that would manufacture the arthritis drug Enbrel. This drug, which had been central to Immunex's future, faced current competing drugs from Johnson & Johnson and Abbott Laboratories, while other potential competitors were in the trial stage. It soon became apparent that Immunex's manufacturing skills were not strong enough to win FDA approval for the facility. As Amgen CEO Kevin Sharer recounted: 'Luckily for us and the patients out there, that's right down Amgen's power alley. We're really good at manufacturing. So I took one of my Executive Committee managers out of his job and said, "You've got one job: Make that factory work and get it licensed." And we did that *before* the deal closed.' In December 2000, several months ahead of some estimates, the plant received FDA approval. By mid-February 2003, all the patients that had been on the waiting list for Enbrel were receiving treatment.

At one level, this is a classic skills synergy: Deep manufacturing capability on the Amgen side of the boundary, and a context in which it could be profitably applied on the Immunex side. However, capturing this skills synergy was not central to the rationale for the deal, and during the due diligence process the full extent of the problems in Rhode Island was not evident. Yet reflection on Amgen's corporate story, in which the development of deep manufacturing skills is an important theme, naturally leads to the question 'Is there any way to draw upon this capability to create value for the merged company?' In this case, there turned out to be a major, urgent opportunity to do so.

What about your partner's corporate story? What value does it bring to the merger? How do you achieve the most valuable result from the two stories coming together?

This may require some imaginative reframing of the combined company's corporate story. Is there, for example, a way of getting past the us-versus-them tensions when two very different companies combine and their future is open?

When France Telecom bought Orange in 2000, Orange's then-CEO Jean-François Pontal found that some of the parent's managers were bristling at the way the acquisition was being described in the business press as a 'reverse takeover'. Pontal countered with a positive metaphor that shifted the emphasis towards what the two sides could accomplish together: 'We bought the Orange brand at a high price, and now we need to *liberate* it so we can get value from it.' So the FT managers had not been taken over at all – they were liberators who would enable their Orange counterparts to accomplish far more than they could have on a freestanding basis.

This was not mere clever rhetoric. It reflected the underlying value logic of the acquisition. Pontal noted that the FT managers quickly recognized the sizeable opportunity involved, so that 'very quickly the old FT mobile operations were no longer waiting for me to tell them to adopt the Orange brand in their countries. They were actually queuing up to be the first to take advantage of the brand.' The key here was to emphasize the future in the corporate story. Managers on both sides of the merger boundary needed to see the promise it held for them. Moreover, for Pontal himself and his team, the framing of the integration as a 'liberation' was helpful in the search for value creation opportunities.

The Sky Chefs case from earlier in this chapter provides yet another example. To be sure, the transformational energy of the acquirer is a valuable part of the story that no one could miss. However, the elevated performance standards that were a part of Sky Chefs' transformation also played an important, if less obvious role. Those standards enabled Kay to turn to his own managers and justify some key appointments in which some of them lost out. It is never easy to apply merit strictly when your company is a dominant acquirer, because your managers will expect to have an edge. A deeply-embedded institutional norm can help to counteract this expectation. Thus the corporate story provided a context within which proven ways of creating value could be applied to new challenges such as a merger.

All these examples involve tailoring the integration in some way based on the relationship between value and people issues. Kaufman, for example, capitalized on the opportunity to improve retention that Arrow's reputation in the industry provided. These examples also illustrate a simple idea that you can share with your team: knowing who we really are tells us a great deal about how we should do the integration. Moreover, adopting the perspective of our various stakeholder groups can help us to understand who we really are. Thus the corporate story is a form of corporate self-knowledge: our knowledge of ourselves in narrative form.

Here again there is no need to depart from the straightforward and powerful language of integration. Just as our interviewees richly employed 'health goals' without ever referring to them as such, so they drew upon their 'corporate stories' without ever using *that* term. Our language is thus like Wittgenstein's ladder: Something you can safely discard once you have climbed up it.

CHAPTER 8

Assuming Personal Leadership

The overwhelming emphasis in this book has been on the *cognitive* challenges of leadership. Paradoxically, however, senior managers often find the *personal change* required to be more taxing than the subtle debates over the merging company's health.

Although this experience can be wrenching, it is rarely emphasized in retrospective accounts of an integration. Oddly, when looking back senior managers tend to tell the merger story in an objective, almost cold form. Others' emotions may be described colorfully, but not the manager's own.

A few of the interviews for this book were conducted in the early stages of an integration, and they capture well what the leader actually experiences. For example, we interviewed Lars Norby, CEO of Group 4 Securicor, towards the beginning of the company's integration. He spoke vividly of a highly personal leadership challenge:

> I believe that it's important that I symbolize the process of integration in my own behavior. This doesn't mean denying my past in one of the two organizations, but rather showing that I no longer represent it. You see, early in the process I have to let down the people on my old side. They naturally see me as their man, but that is no longer the case. I am the new company's man.
>
> And this is all very difficult. My old people come to me to take advantage of the old loyalties and to use the informal communication system we had in place. I have to be alert and apply discipline to avoid giving in to that. And it's hard to get rid of an old identity that I had built up over 15 years.
>
> The difficulty is at a very personal level, because I am outside my comfort zone – the norms and values that made up my old identity and made me feel safe. And although I have hierarchical power in the new company that I need to apply decisively during the integration, I can't just give orders. I also have to lead by showing the change in myself, by demonstrating that I am moving beyond my old role.
>
> And you know that hurts, and people can see that it hurts and that as a leader I'm not invulnerable. But that's a good thing because it

hurts for them too. I don't just mean people that are losing their jobs, but also people that have to switch jobs and even those that just have to change their belief systems a bit. And if they all see me leading outside my comfort zone, I think we have a better chance to build a new company with a new culture.

Unfortunately, some senior leaders do the opposite by retreating into their comfort zones. They may even rationalize to themselves that sticking to their normal routines throughout the integration is actually an effective form of leadership. They are, they think, providing reassurance to employees and other stakeholders who would be disconcerted by changes in the leader's behavior.

There is sometimes an unspoken fear that if they move out of their comfort zone, their leadership actions will be clumsy and therefore ineffective. That is at best half right: clumsy, perhaps, but not ineffective. Employees are much more likely to stretch themselves when they see their leader doing so. One of the great paradoxes of leadership is that a leader's obvious struggles to change may have much more impact than his or her effortless triumphs. It is a paradox that Norby's account captures well.

You cannot lead a merger from inside your comfort zone.

Recognizing the boundaries of one's comfort zone is of course essential for leadership. Effective leadership requires a cohesive and diverse set of interventions, not all of which come naturally to any individual leader. This is a primary theme of all leadership training programs from the entry level on, but the challenge is never fully overcome. In fact, in our experience the senior leaders who have won widespread and deserved praise for their leadership are the most conscious of the constraints imposed on them by the boundaries of their comfort zones. Even though they have steadily broadened these zones over the course of their careers, they know that playing only to their strengths could mean omitting a decisive leadership intervention. This is particularly true during a merger, where profound corporate health implications may demand a variety of interventions.

As this book covers the highly specific application of leadership in mergers, general leadership development lies outside its scope. Moreover, for the developmental challenge of moving outside and expanding one's comfort zone, a book is scarcely the best learning tool. This challenge is best addressed through on-the-job practice, feedback sessions with colleagues and coaches, and the kind of sophisticated modern training that simulates the dangers, discomforts and ambiguities of real leadership. We do, however, have a few practical suggestions to make.

This book has offered many examples of leadership interventions grouped under five leadership challenges. You should be able to identify which of these challenges would be most difficult for you to meet. Or ask a few colleagues to do a forced ranking of them based on how difficult they would be *for you*. Then have a good discussion on why they think so. The same exercise could be done for the specific leadership interventions discussed in this book that are especially relevant for your current integration.

General leadership frameworks have been proliferating since the beginnings of modern management research in the early twentieth century, but there is no general consensus on which is best.[1] It is wise to resort to one with which you and your colleagues are already familiar. Most major corporations have a preferred framework that they use to structure their leadership development. The framework in use at your company might, for example, disaggregate leadership into such activities as raising aspirations, enforcing operational and financial discipline, developing people, fostering change momentum, managing teams, and acting as a role model. What comes easily and what does not? If you have a penchant for enforcing discipline, you might be tempted to spend too much of your time assessing synergy estimates and fail to attend to deteriorating relationships with customers or business partners. If you excel at raising aspirations and fostering change momentum, you may wind up on the rallying the troops while a problem in headquarters such as a dysfunctional top team is undermining the effectiveness of those efforts.

The key here is to undertake your merger leadership role with a clear understanding of the boundaries of your comfort zone. That makes possible the crucial second step: Making a personal commitment to move well outside your comfort zone in several ways, and to call on your team and colleagues to help you to keep that commitment.

What would make up such a commitment? Much here would depend upon the concrete circumstances of the integration, of course, but there are several points that are nearly always essential. In the light of the arguments of this book, in fact, they may seem obvious at this stage, but the decisive factor here is not the understanding to grasp them but rather the emotional toughness to commit to them.

We recommend that you commit to the following:

- *'This will be my baby.'* If you have a first-rate integration manager and team, the temptation to delegate away responsibility for achieving a healthy merger may be very powerful indeed. We do not have space here to dispose of every plausible argument for diverting your time and energies to other items on your agenda. This may, for example, be a terrific opportunity to develop the leadership skills of the managers on the integration team, so that might appear to be a good excuse for backing off. However, your full engagement in the integration process need not hinder others' chances to grow. To the contrary, you should be able to adopt a leadership style that enhances their growth. In short, it can be your baby, and theirs as well.

- *'I am going to aim high with this one.'* Responsibility for the health of the merger will naturally alert you to a host of risks and lead you to take steps to manage them. We have given many examples in this book of where leaders have appropriately done this. Yet every integration – provided that it is not doomed from the start by a flawed strategy or an excessive acquisition premium – offers innumerable opportunities to improve corporate health. Some might be opportunities that the top team has known about for years but has somehow never been ready to tackle. Others may be less obvious, and emerge only during the course of the integration. More often than not these opportunities will require the courage to break some old corporate habits. Success here is almost impossible unless you demonstrate such courage.

- *'I am going back to school on this.'* We focused on the learning topic in the Chapter 6, but the need for it has been implicit throughout the book. Any manager who comes into a senior corporate role from the outside recognizes the need for intensive learning. Unless you are making a small-scale, routine acquisition, a truly new company can and should emerge from the integration process. That means that you and all of your colleagues from both sides are in effect coming as outsiders to this new company. One of the best ways to add value is to persistently focus the attention of both sides on what is *not* known. You should play the role of the intellectual conscience of the integration by defining and pushing a tough learning agenda – with a healthy emphasis on the need for corporate self-knowledge. You should also be the best *listener* in the integration, with your ears ever primed to listen not only to your 'own' people but also to your new colleagues across the merger boundary, your counterparts in other companies, and other informative parties such as customers.

- *'I am going to raise the metabolic rate of this company.'* Healthy mergers require that even hard-driving management teams pick up the pace to the point of discomfort. This is a product of the number of things that need to be decided, and the range of signals that need to be sent. It is true, by the way, even for integrations where there are sound reasons for moving more slowly in sensitive areas. For example, the fact that you are planning to shelter an acquisition from full integration does not mean that the partial integration should be undertaken at a leisurely pace. In general, you should convey a controlled urgency. We have yet to observe a healthy merger without a real sense of hustle.

- *'I am going to achieve absolute authenticity.'* During the integration period, the 'goldfish bowl' aspect of your job will be even more marked than usual. Every action you take should be so strongly consonant with your vision for the new company that widespread knowledge of it could only help your momentum. The best way to become a powerful role model is not to adopt a tactful pose when employees and others are watching, but rather to leave the switch 'on' at all times. There should not be a hair's breadth of difference between the new company values and priorities that you communicate formally and those that you enact every day in every forum. The authenticity that builds new companies depends on who you are and what you do, not just on what you say.

Your chances for success will of course be enhanced if every 'I' in the commitment becomes a 'we' for your entire team. By all means call on your team to share this leadership commitment, but be wary of the insidious temptation to *share it away*. The commitment of a team is no substitute for personal commitment.

All this talk of comfort zones and commitment makes merger leadership sound like a punishing ordeal. It certainly can be a tough experience, but many senior leaders have found it to be one of the best opportunities for personal and professional growth they have had since their exhilarating early days as apprentice managers.

> **Few opportunities to stretch yourself as a leader are as taxing or ultimately rewarding as that provided by a merger.**

Diagnosing the risks and opportunities for corporate health, building a new top team, reconceiving and communicating the corporate story, establishing a performance culture for the new company, engaging with new stakeholders, tackling integration-critical learning and defining a learning agenda for the post-integration period, translating your ideas for a healthy merger into the language of integration, and just coping with the sheer complexity and daunting pace of the integration – all this would stretch the capacities of any general manager. When it comes to leadership development opportunities, this is as good as it gets. Relish it while it lasts.

Chapter 1 The Elusive Healthy Merger

1 Forty years of academic studies confirm that the distribution of 'abnormal returns' (that is, a return for the acquirer that is greater than returns for its competitors) is on average zero. For an acquirer, therefore, the probabilities of creating more or less value than competitors are roughly equal.

2 This question of how to measure merger performance has been the central concern of most formal merger research. Over the years, merger performance has become coupled to the concept of synergies, and this has led to much discussion of which measure is the best proxy for synergy realization. The proposed answers include accounting measures (e.g. variations in ROAs or in cash flows), short-term or long-term stock returns (a few days around the date of the announcement or over three to five years, respectively), and assessments of the degree to which the targeted synergistic benefits have been realized. None of these measures, however, take fully into account the many subtle but profound effects of merger processes on the distinctive advantages the merged company might be accumulating or destroying *vis-à-vis* its competitors. It is even less likely that changes in the quality of the relationships with key external stakeholders (customers, business partners, communities) are targeted and systematically tracked.

Chapter 2 Creating the New Company at the Top

1 By working under a strict confidentiality agreement, members of a 'clean team' secure unrestricted access to data that is legally off-limits to the merging companies' employees before the close. See Nicolas J. Albizzatti, Scott A. Christofferson and Diane L. Sias, 'Smoothing postmerger integration', www.mckinseyquarterly.com, September 2005.

2 The wholesale replacement of the acquired company's top management team is of course fraught with risk. A recent study of US bank mergers shows that this move on average destroys value even where there are strong geographic overlaps (and thus the potential for significant cost efficiencies). See Maurizio Zollo and Harbir Singh, 'Deliberate learning

in corporate acquisitions: Post-acquisition strategies and integration capability in U.S. bank mergers', *Strategic Management Journal*, vol. 25, issue 13, 2004: 1233–56.

3   The noted success of the bottom-up integration planning process used during the SmithKline Beecham merger of 1989 may appear to contradict this point, but it actually supports it. Robert Bauman and Gary Wendt, the two CEOs of the merger partners, ensured early on that the top team achieved a deeply shared vision and a strong sense of identity. The new company thus emerged very quickly at the top. The resulting climate of trust and mutual respect made it possible to delegate the huge task of designing the new company to teams of middle managers. See Robert P. Bauman, Peter Jackson and Joanne T. Lawrence, *From Promise to Performance: A Journey of Transformation at SmithKline Beecham* (Boston: Harvard Business School Press, 1997).

4   Our survey of 161 mergers where McKinsey had an advisory role shows that the timing of the appointment of the top team predicts very well the long-term performance of the combined organization. In general, the earlier the beginning and the end of the decision-making process, the better. Importantly, while an early conclusion of this process matters, the actual length of the process does not.

Chapter 3   Communicating the Corporate Story

1   Increasing the frequency is often touted as a 'silver bullet' solution to communication problems in integrations. However, in our analysis of mergers advised by McKinsey's post-merger management practice we found that it affects merger performance only in specific circumstances and with specific stakeholders. Frequent communication with employees is important, for example, but even more important is the way this communication is carried out: It should be as individualized as possible, with an emphasis on two-way flows of information. Listening is just as important as speaking in merger contexts. Among external audiences, frequent engagement with customers is a key success factor in our data, but not so in the case of other stakeholders. For supply-chain partners and even financial markets, the point of diminishing marginal returns to additional investments in communication might be reached much sooner in most cases. Thus the communications approach must be adapted for each stakeholder group.

For an excellent example on how to lead a highly complex transformational merger of equals with a particularly strong emphasis on developing and communicating the corporate story, see Bauman, Jackson and Lawrence, *op. cit.* For an academic contribution to the understanding of the effects of corporate communication in the post-merger context, see David M. Schweiger and Angelo S. DeNisi, 'Communication with employees following a merger: A longitudinal field experiment', *Academy of Management Journal*, vol. 34, issue 1, 1991: 127–38. For a recent general review of the literature on M&A communications, see Angelo S. DeNisi and Shung-Jae Shen, 'Psychological communication interventions in mergers and acquisitions', in Günter K. Stahl and Mark E. Mendenhall (eds), *Mergers and Acquisitions: Managing Culture and Human Resources* (Stanford: Stanford Business Books, 1989): 228–49.

2   The term 'backstory' is borrowed from screenwriting, where it refers to a character's early history that is not directly narrated on screen but nevertheless has an important influence on how they think and act.

Chapter 4   Establishing a New Performance Culture

1   Learning about a merger partner often throws up important surprises. Recent research shows that the managers of acquired companies are strongly concerned about what the future holds for their parts of the new company. Managers of acquirers may falsely assume that their counterparts are just concerned about their own rewards (power and money). To overlook your partner's keen interest in achieving a healthy merger could lead to a lost opportunity to work together on it. See Melissa Graebner, 'Momentum and serendipity: How acquired leaders create value in the integration of technology firms', *Strategic Management Journal*, 2004, vol. 25, issue 8/9: 751–77; and Melissa Graebner and Kathleen Eisenhardt, 'The seller's side of the story: Acquisition as courtship and governance as syndicate in entrepreneurial firms', *Administrative Science Quarterly*, 2004, vol. 49, issue 3: 366–403.

2   Academic research has looked at the performance implications of differences both in national culture and in organizational culture with mixed results. Differences in national culture between merging firms may not damage performance and in fact may be advantageous. One striking study found, for example, that US companies' acquisitions in Japan and France (where the 'cultural distance' between the countries is great) perform better than those in the UK and Canada. See Anju Seth, Kean P. Song and R. Richardson Pettit, 'Value creation and destruction

in cross-border acquisitions: An empirical analysis', *Strategic Management Journal*, vol. 23, issue 10, 2002: 921–40. In our survey of 161 mergers worldwide where McKinsey played an advisory role we found no performance differences between domestic and cross-border mergers, a result that confirms that differences in national culture are generally manageable.

As for organizational culture, research again does not provide a clear response on the crucial question of whether cultural distance actually hurts merger performance. A few studies find indeed a negative impact. See Sayan Chatterjee, Michael H. Lubatkin, David M. Schweiger and Yaakov Weber, 'Cultural differences and shareholder value in related mergers: Linking equity and human capital', *Strategic Management Journal*, vol. 13, issue 5, 1992: 319–34; and Deepak K. Datta, 'Organizational fit and acquisition performance: Effects of post-acquisition integration', *Strategic Management Journal*, vol. 12, issue 4, 1991: 281–98. However, other studies do not show a negative impact. The most current writings on the subject, in fact, still consider this to be a major paradox. For an updated and extensive treatment of a wide range of topics related to the management of cultural issues in the merger process, see Stahl and Mendenhall, *op. cit.*, chapter 18 of that volume (Günter K. Stahl, Mark E. Mendenhall and Yaakov Weber, 'Research on sociocultural integration in mergers and acquisitions: Points of agreement, paradoxes, and avenues for future research': 401–11) frames the research issues well. One of the reasons for this state of affairs is that researchers have not yet taken the next step by asking under what conditions problems due to cultural distance arise, thus separating them from problems due to inappropriate management of the cultural integration process. Moreover, the impact of specific cultural characteristics of the two organizations has not yet been assessed, so it is not clear whether some organizations are better placed to manage this cultural distance than others, and if so, what traits enable them to do so.

Our survey of 161 mergers suggests that cultural distance between two organizations has no significant impact on the difference between high and low performance. This is in line with the general thrust of the academic literature. Cultural distance, therefore, can be managed through an appropriate mix of content decisions (when cultural gaps should be bridged) and process decisions (how they should be bridged). Most strikingly, our data shows that the cultural dimensions that best explain merger performance are not the differences between the two companies but rather the characteristics of the companies themselves. In the case of acquisitions, the cultural traits of the acquirer are far more important in influencing performance than those of the acquired company are. The traits that matter most are the acquirer's performance orientation, its tolerance of risk, and its tolerance of diversity. These three traits correlate strongly and positively with merger performance.

3 GE Capital's integration approach is described in detail in Ronald N. Ashkenas, Lawrence J. DeMonaco and Suzanne C. Francis, 'Making the deal real: How GE capital integrates acquisitions', *Harvard Business Review*, Jan.–Feb. 1998: 165–78.

4 To establish a new performance culture after a merger, the general principles of organizational change must be applied even though in the special circumstances of an integration the effort will not look like a conventional change program with its open-ended dialogues about the future extending over many weeks or months. McKinsey has developed an 'influence model' that defines the four main forms of leadership intervention which must be combined to secure lasting change in any setting, including mergers: Fostering understanding and conviction (particularly via communication of the corporate story); reinforcing with formal mechanisms (that is, with structures, processes and systems); developing talent and skills; and acting as a role model. In this book much of the emphasis has fallen on the first and fourth forms of intervention, each of which in effect is the main topic of a full chapter (role modeling and the corporate story are central to Chapters 2 and 3, respectively). However, the other two are important as well, as we have seen in this chapter. Michael Kay's intensive coaching of Caterair managers and Dick Evans' detailed definition of management systems for the managers of Alcan's Algroup acquisition are examples. Detailed case analysis of any healthy merger will reveal all four forms of leadership intervention at work, and the leader is responsible for ensuring that they reinforce each other. See Emily Lawson and Colin Price, 'The psychology of change management', *McKinsey Quarterly*, Special Edition: Organization, 2003: 31–41.

Chapter 5 Championing External Stakeholders

1 Any discussion of pricing or territory allocations is of course subject to legal restrictions before the close.

Chapter 6   Fostering Momentum and Learning

1   For an enlightening view on learning across multiple experiences, see Gabriel Szulanski and Sidney Winter, 'Getting it right the second time', *Harvard Business Review*, January 2002: 62–9.

2   The academic literature has largely ignored this key feature of integrations. For the first empirical evidence published in a leading journal, see Christian Homburg and Matthias Bucerius, 'Is speed of integration really a success factor of mergers and acquisitions? An analysis of the role of internal and external relatedness', *Strategic Management Journal*, vol. 27, 2006: 347–67. The article shows that the correlation of speed with performance is not uniform, but rather depends upon the degree to which the two companies are similar across a range of characteristics.

3   Given the well-established importance of learning curves in operating and administrative processes, it is striking that the long months of intensive activity in the typical merger integration do not automatically leave you better prepared for the next integration. For a breakthrough paper on this surprising finding, see Jerayr Haleblian and Sydney Finkelstein, 'The influence of organizational acquisition experience on acquisition performance: A behavioral learning perspective', *Administrative Science Quarterly*, vol. 44, issue 1, 1999: 29–56. Another study shows that prior acquisition experience has no impact on merger performance, whereas the level of investment in learning processes through the development of M&A tools (e.g. integration manuals, decision support systems, etc.) and systematic post-mortem analyses pay back in significantly better performance levels. See Maurizio Zollo and Harbir Singh, 'Deliberate learning in corporate acquisitions: Post-acquisition strategies and integration capability in U.S. bank mergers', *Strategic Management Journal*, vol. 25, issue 13, 2004: 1233–56. See also Matthew L.A. Hayward, 'When do firms learn from their acquisition experience? Evidence from 1990 to 1995', *Strategic Management Journal*, vol. 23, 2002: 21–39.

4   The presence of post-acquisition integration routines explained more than 10 per cent of the variance in merger performance. The presence in the acquirer of a culture for performance and of tolerance of risk and diversity accounted for another 9 per cent and 6.5 per cent, respectively. Together, the three factors explained fully 25 per cent of the variance – an unusually strong result in management research.

5   See Maurizio Zollo, 'Superstitious learning revisited: Outcome ambiguity and confidence traps in corporate acquisitions', INSEAD Working Paper, 2005.

Chapter 7   Mastering the Language of Integration

1   For a book-length assessment of the perils of misplaced confidence in synergy numbers developed during merger negotiations, see Mark L. Sirower, *Synergy Trap: How Companies Lose the Acquisition Game* (New York: The Free Press, 1997).

2   Most published academic and managerial research on post-acquisition management focuses on this problem. For an early and influential treatment, see Philippe C. Haspeslagh and David B. Jemison, *Managing Acquisitions: Creating Value through Corporate Renewal* (New York: Free Press, 1991).

3   For an insightful discussion of some of the hazards to merger success that arise from the way companies handle the internal decision-making process, see David B. Jemison and Sim B. Sitkin, 'Acquisitions: The process can be a problem', *Harvard Business Review*, March–April 1986: 107–16. The authors argue that often the chief problem is not in what we do – for example, in the content of integration decisions – but in the way we go about doing it.

4   See Matthias Bekier and Michael J. Shelton, 'Keeping your sales force after the merger', *McKinsey Quarterly*, 2002, no. 4: 106–15.

5   Research has shown that there are subtle trade-offs that need to be carefully weighed. In a recent study of acquisitions of high-tech start-ups, the level of integration of the acquired unit was found to be *negatively* related to the likelihood of launching the first post-merger product. However, higher levels of integration were also *positively* linked to the number of subsequent product launches. In other words, leaving high levels of autonomy to acquired technology companies might seem to be the right thing to do for the immediate time horizon, but the same decision can hurt in more subtle ways the ability of the merged company to combine complementary skills to foster long-term innovation. See Phanish Puranam, Harbir Singh and Maurizio Zollo, 'Organizing for innovation: Managing the coordination-autonomy dilemma in technology acquisitions', *Academy of Management Journal*, vol. 49, issue 2, 2006: 263–80.

6   For a powerful example of this trade-off, see Bauman, Jackson and Lawrence, *op. cit.* In this 1989 merger, the two CEOs intentionally slowed down the integration decision-making process in order to allow the task forces to generate integration plans in a genuinely bottom-up way. Time was ultimately made up through an extremely rapid execution that proceeded almost flawlessly despite the high complexity of the merger.

7   In less excited tones, the academic literature underscores the importance of people issues. For example, there is significant evidence that replacement of senior managers in an acquired company increases the risk of value destruction. This finding holds even in integrations focused on cost efficiencies. See Albert Cannella and Don Hambrick, 'Effects of executive departures on the performance of acquired firms', *Strategic Management Journal*, vol. 14, Special Issue, 1993: 137–52.

8   The literature on the people issues of mergers is large and growing. For a classic early framing of the issues, see Anthony F. Buono and James L. Bowditch, *The Human Side of Mergers and Acquisitions: Managing Collisions between People, Cultures, and Organizations* (San Francisco: Jossey-Bass, 1989).

9   Haspeslagh and Jemison, *op. cit.*, offered an early and influential integration typology. They distinguished between 'absorption', 'preservation' and 'symbiotic' integration approaches, driven by the level of strategic interdependence between the two companies and by the degree to which autonomy must be provided to the acquired one in order to protect its ability to create value. For a more recent integration typology, see Joseph L. Bower, 'Not all M&As are alike – and that matters', *Harvard Business Review*, March 2001: 93–101.

10   It is obvious to experienced managers that overconfidence can be dangerous, but research underscores the startling severity of this trap. A recent study looked at how performance assessments of prior acquisitions correlated with the likelihood of success of current ones. The study found a strong *negative* correlation between how well managers think they did in the past, and how well they will actually do in the current merger. Even more interestingly, the negative correlation actually *increases* as acquisition experience accumulates. Evidently, having implemented many mergers in the past is taken as evidence of strong integration capabilities, and the resulting growth in self-confidence has negative effects on the current merger that outweigh the positive value of the actual learning from experience. See Zollo, *op. cit.*

Chapter 8   Assuming Personal Leadership

1   Given the numerous general frameworks in use, it is remarkable how little has been written by academic researchers specifically on *merger* leadership. A merger-specific leadership framework is outlined in Sim B. Sitkin, and Amy L. Pablo, 'The neglected importance of leadership

in mergers and acquisitions' in Amy L. Pablo and Mansour Javidan (eds), *Mergers and Acquisitions: Creating Integrative Knowledge* (Malden, MA: Blackwell Publishing, 2004): 209–23. This framework in turn draws upon the general leadership framework offered in Sim B. Sitkin, E. Allan Lind and Christopher P. Long, *The Pyramidal Model of Leadership* (Durham, NC: Duke University Press, 2001).

Albizzatti, Nicolas J., Scott A. Christofferson and Diane L. Sias, 'Smoothing post-merger integration', www.mckinseyquarterly.com, September 2005.

Ashkenas, Ronald N., Lawrence J. DeMonaco and Suzanne C. Francis (1998) 'Making the deal real: How GE capital integrates acquisitions', *Harvard Business Review*, Jan.–Feb.: 165–78.

Bauman, Robert P., Peter Jackson and Joanne T. Lawrence (1997) *From Promise to Performance: A Journey of Transformation at SmithKline Beecham* (Boston: Harvard Business School Press).

Bekier, Matthias and Michael J. Shelton (2002) 'Keeping your sales force after the merger', *McKinsey Quarterly*, 2002, no. 4: 106–15.

Bower, Joseph L. (2001) 'Not all M&As are alike – and that matters', *Harvard Business Review*, March: 93–101.

Buono, Anthony F. and James L. Bowditch (1989) *The Human Side of Mergers and Acquisitions: Managing Collisions between People, Cultures, and Organizations* (San Francisco: Jossey-Bass).

Cannella, Albert and Don Hambrick (1993) 'Effects of executive departures on the performance of acquired firms', *Strategic Management Journal*, vol. 14, Special Issue: 137–52.

Chatterjee, Sayan, Michael H. Lubatkin, David M. Schweiger and Yaakov Weber (1992) 'Cultural differences and shareholder value in related mergers: Linking equity and human capital', *Strategic Management Journal*, vol. 13, issue 5: 319–34.

Datta, Deepak K. (1991) 'Organizational fit and acquisition performance: Effects of post-acquisition integration', *Strategic Management Journal*, vol. 12, issue 4: 281–98.

DeNisi, Angelo S. and Shung-Jae Shen (1989) 'Psychological communication interventions in mergers and acquisitions', in Günter K. Stahl and Mark E. Mendenhall (eds), *Mergers and Acquisitions: Managing Culture and Human Resources* (Stanford: Stanford Business Books): 228–49.

Graebner, Melissa (2004) 'Momentum and serendipity: How acquired leaders create value in the integration of technology firms', *Strategic Management Journal*, vol. 25, issue 8/9: 751–77.

Graebner, Melissa and Kathleen Eisenhardt (2004) 'The seller's side of the story: Acquisition as courtship and governance as syndicate in entrepreneurial firms', *Administrative Science Quarterly*, vol. 49, issue 3: 366–403.

Haleblian, Jerayr and Sydney Finkelstein (1999) 'The influence of organizational acquisition experience on acquisition performance: A behavioral learning perspective', *Administrative Science Quarterly*, vol. 44, issue 1: 29–56.

Haspeslagh, Philippe C. and David B. Jemison (1991) *Managing Acquisitions: Creating Value through Corporate Renewal* (New York: Free Press).

Hayward, Matthew L.A. (2002) 'When do firms learn from their acquisition experience? Evidence from 1990 to 1995', *Strategic Management Journal*, vol. 23: 21–39.

Homburg, Christian and Matthias Bucerius (2006) 'Is speed of integration really a success factor of mergers and acquisitions? An analysis of the role of internal and external relatedness', *Strategic Management Journal*, vol. 27: 347–67.

Jemison, David B. and Sim B. Sitkin (1986) 'Acquisitions: The process can be a problem', *Harvard Business Review*, March–April: 107–16.

Lawson, Emily and Colin Price (2003) 'The psychology of change management', *McKinsey Quarterly*, Special Edition: Organization: 31–41.

Sitkin, Sim B. and Amy L. Pablo (2004) 'The neglected importance of leadership in mergers and acquisitions', in Amy L. Pablo and Mansour Javidan (eds), *Mergers and Acquisitions: Creating Integrative Knowledge* (Malden, MA: Blackwell Publishing): 209–23.

Puranam, Phanish, Harbir Singh and Maurizio Zollo (2005) 'Organizing for innovation: Managing the coordination-autonomy dilemma in technology acquisitions', *Academy of Management Journal*, vol. 49, issue 2, 2006: 263–80.

Schweiger, David M. and Angelo S. DeNisi (1991) 'Communication with employees following a merger: A longitudinal field experiment', *Academy of Management Journal*, vol. 34, issue 1: 127–38.

Seth, Anju, Kean P. Song and R. Richardson Pettit (2002) 'Value creation and destruction in cross-border acquisitions: An empirical analysis', *Strategic Management Journal*, vol. 23, issue 10: 921–40.

Sirower, Mark L. (1997) *Synergy Trap: How Companies Lose the Acquisition Game* (New York: The Free Press).

Sitkin, Sim B., E. Allan Lind and Christopher P. Long (2001) *The Pyramidal Model of Leadership* (Durham, NC: Duke University Press).

Stahl, Günter K. and Mark E. Mendenhall (eds) (1989) *Mergers and Acquisitions: Managing Culture and Human Resources* (Stanford: Stanford Business Books).

Stahl, Günter K., Mark E. Mendenhall and Yaakov Weber (1989) 'Research on sociocultural integration in mergers and acquisitions: Points of agreement, paradoxes, and avenues for future research', in Günter K. Stahl and Mark E. Mendenhall (eds), *Mergers and Acquisitions: Managing Culture and Human Resources* (Stanford: Stanford Business Books): 401–11.

Szulanski, Gabriel and Sidney Winter (2002) 'Getting it right the second time', *Harvard Business Review*, January: 62–9.

Zollo, Maurizio and Harbir Singh (2004) 'Deliberate learning in corporate acquisitions: Post-acquisition strategies and integration capability in U.S. bank mergers', *Strategic Management Journal*, vol. 25, issue 13: 1233–56.

Zollo, Maurizio (2005) 'Superstitious learning revisited: Outcome ambiguity and confidence traps in corporate acquisitions', INSEAD Working Paper.

Note: interviewees are listed under their affiliated companies.